PRAYING THE BIBLE

PRAYING THE BIBLE
A PARISH LIFE SOURCEBOOK

Elizabeth Canham
Preface by James C. Fenhagen

COWLEY PUBLICATIONS
CAMBRIDGE, MASSACHUSETTS

Published in the United States of America by Cowley
Publications.

International Standard Book No.: 0-936384-46-8

Library of Congress Cataloging-in-Publication Data

Canham, Elizabeth, 1939–
   Praying the Bible.

   (Parish life sourcebooks)
   1. Bible--Devotional use. 2. Prayer. I. Title.
II. Series.
BS617.8.C36 1987   248.3   86-32976
ISBN 0-936384-46-8

Cowley Publications
980 Memorial Drive
Cambridge, MA 02138

For Marjorie

FOREWORD

Books on Christian spirituality make their connection with their readers not so much on their erudition as on their ability to illuminate human experience. There have been many thoughtful and well-written books about the life of prayer that I have not responded to simply because their approach reflects concerns and questions which have not been my own. When I picked up Elizabeth Canham's new book, therefore, I did so with this question of connection lurking in the back of my mind. But to my surprise, even before the question was articulated, the connection was made. I was excited by what I was reading. The questions she was asking and the emphases which were important to her were important to me also.

Praying the Bible is written for anyone who is serious about Christian prayer. It is simple enough to challenge the beginners, and reflective enough to stimulate those who have given this area of life a lot of attention. It is short, well-written and designed to be read both by individuals and groups who want to venture further into life in Christ. The chapter headings indicate the flavor of what they contain: Bearing the Wound, Praying the Psalms, Knowing the Scriptures, Hearing the Word, Seeing the Lord and Living the Questions. As is suggested, the approach to the spiritual life which Elizabeth Canham takes is open-ended, rigorously honest, and evocative rather than didactic.

Since in my own life I spend a lot of time with the Psalms, I was particularly grateful for the way in which the Psalms were explored as an avenue to prayer. They are approached critically and then personally. "Our knowledge of the universe has expanded far beyond the ancient world view represented in the

Psalm, " she writes, but, "Can we not look at the dancing light and movement of the clouds and lift our hearts in praise of the creator who enlightens our minds?" Or again, "The Psalms invite us to be honest . . . . The imprecatory Psalms have a therapeutic quality to them because in the expression of howling rage I am led to new perspectives of how things actually are and the assurance that God has not abandoned me because I did not meet my own standards of Christian perfection."

Elizabeth Canham's *Praying the Bible* is a thoughtful and helpful book for anyone who is serious about the life of prayer. It takes familiar themes and opens them to fresh insight. I began the book hesitantly but did not stop until I finished, and to my surprise, *Praying the Bible* is a book I have already gone back to again.

James C. Fenhagen
General Theological Seminary

ACKNOWLEDGEMENTS

Many people have contributed to the writing of this book as their lives have touched mine. I am grateful to Avery Brooke, who first suggested the title, and offered much encouragement along the way. Seminarians at Wilson Carlisle College in London, the General Theological Seminary, and New York Theological Seminary in the U.S.A., have stimulated and suggested much of the material as we worked together.

I wish also to express my thanks to the Order of the Holy Cross for the many invitations to conduct workshops and retreats on Prayer and the Bible, and to share its life. Special gratitude is due to the Community at Holy Savior Priory—Bede, Ray, Tom, Nick, Frank and Georgia—for their patience and support during the final stages of writing the manuscript.

To all the unnamed friends and colleagues who have contributed to this book, I offer thanks. Their willingness to dialogue, challenge and affirm has helped to shape my ideas, and to stimulate further thought.

AUTHOR'S PREFACE

How can we, who live in a post-critical era, recapture the delight our forebears found in the well-known and much loved Scriptures? Can we "pray the Bible" in our time? These questions will be addressed both through an evaluation of current approaches to the Bible and in the light of tradition. The last century has witnessed a revolution in our study of the biblical literature and two extreme positions have emerged among Christians. There are those whose critical/academic analysis of the Bible has led them to view it with a scepticism that precludes devotional use. The other group totally rejects current scholarship and retreats to a fundamentalism which results in an uncritical devotional approach and frequently uses the language and images of a past era. Both positions fail to do justice to the living Word of God who is never obsolete.

Some clues to the solution of our contemporary problem may be forthcoming as we consider the past. How did the Hebrews "pray the Bible"? They certainly were familiar with its content in a way few of us are, and learned to "meditate on it day and night." Corporate prayer was the foundation undergirding personal prayer, and this was basic also to the early Christian communities. The Psalms, which so powerfully encapsulate the extremes of human emotion and experience, are profoundly relevant for our prayers. So are the lives of God's people whose stories reveal the hope and doubt, joy and pain, growth and stagnation which are part of our lives too. We will read their stories with fresh insight as we enter into dialogue with the sacred text that tells us how life was for them. I am convinced that an existential approach, which allows the Scriptures to stand in their own context, which questions, evaluates, analyses, but also permits God to address *us* in our time through them, is the most satisfactory way of praying the Bible now. Some practical suggestions will be offered to facilitate both individuals and groups to approach the Bible in this way.

CONTENTS

BEARING THE WOUND

he dreamed on in curves
and equations
with the smell of saltpetre
in his nostrils, and saw the hole
in God's side that is the wound
of knowledge and
thrust his hand in it and believed.[1]

Those who are familiar with the King James version of the Bible will recall that in his farewell discourses (John 14-17) Jesus promised to send "another comforter" to be with the disciples after his departure. Today's reader might entertain warm, contented feelings when reading that passage. The translators of the King James version had no such thoughts. In the seventeenth century a comforter was a goad, a means of prodding reluctant servants or animals into action. So the Holy Spirit was not being defined as the bringer of peace and tranquility in the absence of Jesus, but as a disturbing, insistent spur, pressing the disciples into action. I am told that a similar use of the word comfort may be seen in the Bayeux Tapestry in France. Under a section in which King Harold is depicted riding into battle carrying a lance with which he is prodding his troops, the caption reads: "Harold comforts his troops"!

Many twentieth century Christians who felt supported by these verses have been resistant to other translations of the original Greek word, *parakletos*. Such alternatives as *Counselor*, *Advocate*, or the transliteration *Paraclete* are rejected because they lack the warmth and comfort of the more familiar term. Several important issues are raised by this reaction to variation in Biblical interpretation. First it highlights the fact that most of us dislike what is new and unfamiliar. We resist change, especially when it challenges the assumptions on which our faith has

1

been constructed. Secondly, it reflects our predisposition to give to words—even the words of Scripture—the meaning they have for us, and this may be far removed from their original context. Thirdly, if we read and seriously attempt to understand the Bible, God will disturb us into taking new risks of faith, and our understanding will influence our praying.

The last century has witnessed an unprecedented growth in human knowledge and achievement. We have walked on the moon, plumbed the depths of the human psyche, explored our origins and learned how to destroy the earth at the touch of a button. Developments in theology, the "Queen of Sciences," have been no less robust. From Graf-Wellhausen through Schweitzer, Bultmann, Kung and Schillebeeckx, the Bible has been subjected to critical analysis. The sacred Scriptures have been dissected and examined in the light of fresh archaeological, psychological, sociological and linguistic data. Many devout Christians in this post-Darwinian, post-Freudian era feel that their most treasured possession has been wrested from them. Others react differently. Ostrich-like, they retreat into a biblical literalism which refuses to allow any of these influences to impinge upon their belief system.

Most contemporary Christians probably find themselves in that grey area between these two positions. Few really know the Bible well, apart from a selection of well-marked passages which have been useful at crisis points in their lives. Gone are the days of systematic, rote learning of the Bible in Sunday School, and although some of today's Christian believers are aware that there have been considerable developments in the area of biblical knowledge and interpretation, they are not informed about them. Even if they want to explore the Bible for themselves, they may be intimidated by their lack of expertise in these new disciplines.

The training of prospective clergy includes introduction to biblical criticism, exegesis and homiletics. To some the challenge of assimilating new approaches to biblical literature is a severe one, and many seminarians experience a crisis of faith. The often hard-won struggle to accept a vocation to ministry is shattered by the discovery that faith has been built on shaky foundations. The new knowledge received inflicts a wound, which may be experienced as a sickness from which recovery is uncertain. Questions are raised, paradoxes uncovered, ambiguity increases—and it hurts. If, instead of refusing loss of the illusion of certainty and fixed assumptions, we consent to this process of stripping which places us in question, we learn to know God who is Mystery. Such knowledge brings exquisite joy and intense pain.

The poetry of R.S. Thomas, from which the title of this chapter is taken, embodies the willingness to live life's dilemmas. Thomas, in love with nature and God, questions and challenges the incongruities of human experience. He can write of the wound of knowledge because he has been wounded by the kind of knowing that continually opens up new questions. As a priest he struggled with issues that compelled him to be real about his believing.

How can prospective clergy be of assistance to others searching for God when their own God-experience is in question? How can prayers have meaning or the Bible be a source of devotion when its trustworthiness is questioned? One possible solution, and a substantial number opt for this, is to distinguish between the academic and devotional reading of Scripture. For the purpose of passing examinations and satisfying professors, the analytical, critical work is accomplished with mechanical accuracy, but in the seminarian's personal prayers and devotional reading this approach is abandoned in favor of an earlier precritical relation to the text. Thus a kind of schizophrenic, compartmentalizing of approaches is established, and is often carried from seminary classroom to pulpit. The assumption here is that the laity cannot be expected to deal with the difficult struggle for meaning which their pastor has not resolved.

In some cases the faith crisis is dealt with by simply abandoning faith in the traditional sense. The academic and critical approach to Scripture becomes an all-consuming absorption, fascinating in and of itself, and its own goal. Believing becomes an intellectual exercise to be supported by rational processes and freed from the subjective dangers of feeling and emotion. Of those who take this path a number will decide that parish ministry is not for them, and they will opt for an academic career or a minimum involvement with the church, while pursuing another profession. My own formative years were spent in an Evangelical Free Church in England where the Bible was revered as the authoritative, inerrant Word of God. Sunday sermons were long and heavily biblical, and all serious Church members were expected to be present at the weekly Bible study. No critical study of the text was permitted, for this represented a blasphemous approach to the sacred Scriptures. Interpretation was rigidly conservative, drawing its inspiration from John Calvin and the Puritans. The result of this formation was threefold. I found in biblical fundamentalism both an authoritative support system and certainty in matters of faith constructed on an infallible Bible. I learned to know the Scriptures well and immersed myself in serious study of the text. And I learned to love these writings and the God I perceived through them.

There came a time however, when I could no longer maintain that approach to Scripture with integrity. The tensions and dichotomies described in this chapter were reflected in my experience as I struggled with a desire for the familiar and with the invitation to risk new thinking. Although my own faith journey has led me to relinquish biblical fundamentalism, I remain indebted to those who inspired and nurtured my love for the

Scriptures. That love is like an intoxicant; I am "hooked" by the Bible and as my knowledge grows, there is a constant shattering of the inadequate images in which I construct the Creator. For God is Mystery, inviting me in these sacred pages to take off my shoes, and stand silent on this holy ground. God is always beyond my imaginings, yet inexplicably present, infusing me with hunger for the Word which gives life.

Yet the price of synthesis was iconoclasm. Seminary plunged me into the world of academic theology, where biblical criticism was the prerequisite for university graduation. At first I tried the ostrich approach. This was not too difficult to begin with, since I really did believe that what I had been taught earlier was right, and that the academic theologians were not on the side of truth. I managed to suppress doubts when the results of critical analysis seemed more plausible than literalism, and as a result the schizophrenic syndrome began. It lasted several years, at one time almost resulting in an abandonment of faith altogether. Only when I was ready to face the fear of loss—loss of certainty, external affirmation, an infallible Bible and a cherished support system—did the idols begin to shatter. It was a period of darkness, disorientation and doubt, yet, paradoxically, a time in which I knew that God *is* more profoundly than ever before.

I could no longer, with integrity, claim that the Bible was inerrant, yet the essential truth of the Scriptures became more alive and real as I let go of fear. Gone was the need for intellectual gymnastics to "prove" that God created the world in six days (and placed fossils in the soil to confuse us!). The two different, and sometimes conflicting, stories of creation in the opening chapters of Genesis yielded far richer meaning as I allowed them to speak for themselves without imposing twentieth century scientific analysis upon them. Now I found a loving God smiling as each new phase of creation took place and saying "Behold, it is very good." This God, who celebrates the wonder of all that is made, including men and women created together in the divine image, also gave to them stewardship of the earth. The newness of such an insight, the wonder and responsibility of it, exploded into my consciousness and then into my prayers. Because of this insight I could no longer be a passive observer of the rape of the earth, the inequitable distribution of its produce, or the oppression of many of its people. This God involved me in an on-going process of caring for and redeeming the world so that once again the proclamation, "Behold, it is very good," might be made. Such prayerful and praiseful response never came from endless debates defending God against the scientists.

Academic study of the New Testament taught me there is no guarantee that we have, verbatim, the actual words of Jesus. After all no one was around with a tape recorder when the first gospel came into written form some twenty-five years after the death of Jesus. So what was left—if even this part of the sacred text was open to question? We have inherited the accounts of the life and teaching of Jesus written by men whose lives were transformed by him. They write from a post-resurrection perspective and after years of reflection. By that time some of their confusion about Jesus had cleared. They had come to know the Christ of faith, to live their way into the teaching of the historical Jesus and to discover the enduring quality of his life. And they record the words they remember and that the oral tradition had preserved. They record the essential, life-changing message of Jesus, and they do so not out of a Western compulsion for linguistic accuracy, but from the experience of being transformed by it.

I began to read the Gospel not out of fear because the inerrant words of Christ had been taken from me, but believing that the eternal Word speaks in and beyond the written account. "Who do people say that I am?" Jesus asks his disciples at Caesarea Philippi, and they offer a variety of conjectures—John the Baptist, Elijah, one of the prophets. "But who do you say that I am?" They must make their own response, confess him and subsequently come to understand the less palatable dimensions of the statement of faith. It is Peter who answers for them, "You are the Christ," and soon they hear that even this answer is incomplete; their understanding of the nature of Messiahship is inadequate. They want glory, but his glory is to be made manifest through suffering. By the time the story was written in the gospels, the writers had learned for themselves that discipleship was not a comfortable option. As I read the story I hear the question in my own time and context: "Who do you say that I am?" Biblical criticism has not robbed me of the voice of God. Instead I am compelled to search for my own answer, and to relinquish the projections I make of a comfortable Christ figure who will not disturb me. I need to say who Jesus is for me again and again, at ever deepening levels of experience.

Critical analysis of the Scriptures and their devotional use need not conflict with one another. The author of St. John's gospel tells us that Jesus said "I am the truth," and that his purpose is to lead us into all truth. We need not fear that the truth will be lost if the insights of current scholarship are allowed to challenge our interpretation of the Bible. We may be made uncomfortable at times, we may not like what we learn if our cherished images are broken, but if we are willing to be confused, questioned, and stimulated into new ways of thinking the Scriptures will become even more alive to us. Personally I found the movement from disintegration to synthesis was painful, prolonged and richly rewarding. The journey continues, and current idols will need to be shattered as new possibilities present themselves to me. Undoubtedly we will resist each new iconoclasm. The Spirit of God is constantly working, goading me along fresh paths, compelling me to stretch and grow into a faith that is robust.

For many people the problem of Bible interpretation lies not in too much critical analysis but in their lack of academic study. They are not sure how to begin, not sure if they will get it right, and anxious about meddling with the Scriptures. Chapter 3 addresses this difficulty in some detail but it is important to recognize and comment upon it here. Our preoccupation with orthodoxy (right doctrine) generates anxiety when it comes to reading the Bible and making connections with it. Church councils make pronouncements on what we should believe; we have our creeds and confessions of faith, all designed to help us get our thinking straight. Those who publicly deviate from this body of doctrine may be subjected to ecclesiastical discipline or even expulsion from the church. How can the average church member read and correctly interpret the Bible? Surely we should leave that to the experts! An important, fresh approach to biblical interpretation has emerged among Third World Christians, especially in Latin America. Liberation Theology, as it is called, is a process of setting people free from the constraints of oppression whether they be religious, political or racial. The primary concern is not with orthodoxy but with "ortho-praxis," a term which means to work out and *practice* the implications of Christian faith. The question is less "What do you believe?" and more "How do you live?" Right conduct is crucial. Perhaps a greater concern for orthopraxis (right practice) will help overcome reticence about engaging with the Scriptures and the methodology of liberation theology, especially as this has evolved in Latin America, can help us.

The abstract approach of much Western theology has little appeal for the majority in Latin America who are poor and oppressed. They are not much interested in the various arguments for the existence of God which occupied many seminary hours for most clergy. Instead they are concerned about having enough to eat, about a decent place to live, and about the dignity of human labor. Most do not have an advanced education and many are illiterate, so the question of reading and interpreting the Bible "correctly" is difficult. For many the Church has lost credibility, since often it appeared to be associated with a wealthy oligarchy and to be offering redress for the imbalances of society only in an afterlife. It was doing little to alleviate present suffering and the hungry could not eat platitudes. Out of the soil of inequity liberation theology grew and people began to learn that the Gospel of Jesus Christ is about freedom and justice. What is more, they began to realize that they could be involved in bringing it about.

Liberation theology is highly contextual. It begins with an analysis of society and goes on to ask how the Scriptures relate to the status quo. In Latin America people observed that a small number of very wealthy people held power over a growing number of poor. It also became obvious that most commodities, including theology, were imported and therefore foreign. Another unhappy discovery was that aid and investment from wealthy countries often resulted in loss of jobs for the peasant farmers and that profits went to the multi-national companies who were there to "help." Did the Scriptures have anything to say which could give hope in this situation? In order to respond to this question, intentional communities began to form and to study the Bible from their own perspective. The priest no longer functioned as the authority figure who had the answers and could tell people how and what to believe. Instead he became the facilitator of a process in which each person learned to do theology. Often the biblical accounts were being heard for the first time, and their was an air of excitement as people made their own connections with the text. Even well-known stories took on a new dimension. The beaten up person lying by the side of the road who was passed by when a priest and a Levite came along, but was cared for by a despised Samaritan, could be identified with the poor who were beaten up by this society. Those who might be expected to help, respected leaders with resources, ignored the plight of the victim. Who then was the helper? The compassionate one was, himself, despised and marginalized by society, and it was easy for the poor of Latin America to see themselves in the Samaritan. *They* could support and help each other by coming together and expressing solidarity as they pooled their resources. The Gospel gave them an impetus for self-help, and cooperatives of various kinds sprang out of their reading and applying the Scriptures. This is orthopraxis—right action to alleviate distress and resist oppression. Like the Israelites leaving bondage in Egypt the Word of the Lord came to them, enabling them to let go of passivity and hopelessness and to claim their freedom.

It would be inappropriate for those of us living outside Latin America simply to take over the conclusions of liberation theology in that society. Our task is to engage with the same seriousness in an analysis of our own society and then to allow the Scriptures to address us where we are. Simply to discover what they meant in the days of Jesus will not do. It is possible to be a highly skilled academic theologian, expert in exegesis, without making application of the Bible to daily life. Equally the person who has received little or no Bible training is able to relate the message of the Scriptures to contemporary situations in the most insightful way, given encouragement and support. True education consists in the drawing out and validation of the wisdom deep within each person, but we have turned that concept on its head in attempting to fill the learner with more information from kindergarten to graduate school. When we allow for the innate capacity to made connections, when we share insight instead of locating wisdom in a few experts to whom we give power and authority, then community building can begin and the liberating Gospel is heard in our time and place.

This kind of approach to the Bible also alleviates some of the difficulties experienced when we try to read a document written in a vastly different time and culture. Making connections with the Scriptures and our own experience often leads to a desire to dig into the background in order to understand more fully and respond more effectively. But that is not a prerequisite for study. Rather, the energy for further investigation flows from a sense of the contemporary nature of the Scriptures and their importance for our lives. The Word of God is the seed scattered in the soil of human lives. Sometimes it falls upon the hard pathway, where it cannot take root but is consumed by the birds of busyness, tiredness, and boredom. When this happens we do not pray the Bible because its treasure is quickly snatched from us. It has only briefly touched the hard parts of our lives. Sometimes it falls in the shallow places and though our enthusiasm may cause an initial growth, its effectiveness is quickly lost. It dies because we resisted the effort to dig deep in order to get beyond the hard core of bedrock, opting instead for superficial religious experience. Some seed falling among the weeds that we are unwilling to root out will be strangled by their tendrils. God's truth and our unreality may look deceptively similar, but ultimately one of them will die. Sometimes we may be deceived into imagining the weeds we cultivate are essentials of faith, while God invites us to uproot them so that in the darkness of uncertainty the real seed can grow. But the Gospel tells us that some seed will be planted in soil well prepared; in good earth filled with nutrients. Any gardener will confirm that time, study, and effort are required before the ground is ready to receive the seed which will grow into a harvest. And Jesus seemed to understand it, too, when he told this powerful little parable about the living Word of God. All four possibilities exist in each of us; how we receive the Word will determine how we pray it—and if we pray it. God's purpose is harvest. Our response to the seed gift is part

PRAYING THE PSALMS

Hallelujah!
Sing to the Lord a new song;
sing his praise in the congregation of the faithful.
(Ps. 149:1)

All the extremes of human experience are encapsulated in the Psalms. These songs of God's ancient people express yearning and joy, vengeance and love, rage and calm serenity, dereliction and a sense of the all-embracing presence of the Lord. Through the Psalms the Israelites wept together, celebrated victory, danced and made music, lamented and found hope in Yahweh—the God they sometimes doubted and sometimes felt close to. The Psalter has been cherished down through the centuries by both Judaism and Christianity, and it is a good starting point for praying the Bible since the Psalms *are* prayers.

The worship of ancient Israel was centered in the Temple at Jerusalem, where a complex order of ministers, sacrifices and other ritual developed. The psalms are the cult songs that accompanied this worship, many of them written to celebrate some specific event in Israel's history. Others have a prior existence, for they were taken over and adapted from yet more ancient sources. Psalm 104, for example, closely resembles a hymn addressed to Aton, the solar diety of Egypt in the second millennium B. C. No doubt influences from early Egyptian worship were absorbed by the Canaanites against whom the Hebrews waged constant battle. Although Israel displaced them territorially, and the prophetic voice was frequently raised against compromise, many Canaanite ideas passed over into Hebrew thought. Psalm 104 may well provide an example of this, though the theology of the Psalm over all is distinctively Hebrew. It is a song of rare beauty in praise of the Creator God who, in Genesis 1, pronounces that all is very good.

13

Bless the Lord, O my soul;
O Lord my God, how excellent is your greatness!
You are clothed with majesty and splendor.
You wrap yourself in light as with a cloak
and spread out the heavens like a curtain.
You lay the beams of your chambers in the waters above;
You make the clouds your chariot;
you ride on the wings of the wind. (Ps. 104:1-3)

Psalm 104 upholds a pre-scientific view of the universe. The earth rests on pillars and is covered by a dome containing windows, which open to allow rain to fall. Over much of the world there is water and between the foundations on which the earth rests, the waters of the deep are located. God, who is represented in anthropomorphic terms, has the beams of his chambers in the waters above the heavens. His presence is known through the cloak of light surrounding him and he rides on a cloudy chariot sending winds as his messengers. Everything in creation has its time and place, and all things depend on Yahweh, who is all powerful.

All of them look to you
to give them their food in due season. (Ps. 104:28)

It is possible to read this Psalm from a critical perspective, analyze its origins, and reject its primitive imagery. Some readers may even question the appropriateness of using material which has "pagan" sources. In other words, the step by step analytical approach appears to rob the Psalm of its usefulness as a devotional tool. This need not be so. Whenever we speak of God we use images, since there is no other way to communicate about the One who is Mystery. Our knowledge of the universe has expanded far beyond the ancient world view represented in the Psalm, but its symbolic language and the myth it embraces express truth still rich in meaning for us. Can we not look at the dancing light and movement of the clouds, and lift our hearts in praise of the Creator who enlightens our minds? Can we not stand awestruck, watching waves crash against the rocks or the tide gently lapping a sandy shore, and rejoice in the mystery of its limits? As we watch birds nest building, observe each little creature in its habitat, are we not drawn in wonder to give thanks for all that God has made? And what about the food which sustains us and the wine which makes us glad, are not these also gifts that a loving Creator provides with our cooperation and for which we give joyful praise, even though they may have come to us pre-packaged from the supermarket?

In the previous chapter we considered the question of whether biblical criticism might rob us of the capacity to read Scripture devotionally. Here we see that knowing more about the origin of the Psalm, and understanding its pre-scientific context, in fact expands our ability to connect with it. When we let go of our demand for scientific, historical accuracy the poetry of the Psalms heightens our consciousness and moves us to worship. It intensifies our worship of the God we know so partially, and teaches us to celebrate the mystery of God's being which is both hidden and revealed in all things.

Like the Hebrew people Christians have incorporated the Psalms in worship, especially in those churches which have a strong liturgical tradition. Thus the Psalter continues to be used as a corporate expression of prayer even by those whose sense of community and national identity is vastly different from that of the Hebrews. Some of the original impact may be lost to us but we invest these songs of ancient Israel with our own meaning. We allow them to express our feelings and to tell our stories. By approaching them existentially, that is, from where we actually are now, they continue to live in our time and help us to know our roots. We pray with and through the literature of the past as we relate to the eternal God in our present.

The Psalms have long been used in personal prayer, and although this may be a form of praying very different from their original context, it is no less valid. Countless Christians have derived comfort from the recitation of the 23rd Psalm even though they may pray it in a crowded city suburb far removed from rural Israel, pastures and shepherds. In our personal journey of faith we sometimes know loneliness and a sense of exile which can be expressed by the lament of Israel in Babylon, though we are praying at home or in our own backyard. And we do not need to gaze at the Golan Heights in order to lift our eyes to the mountains, recognizing that our help comes from the Lord, Maker of heaven and earth. In company with God's people at worship, or alone in our own room we can express our prayer through the songs of the early Hebrews.

The Psalms invite us to be honest. Many Christians have great difficulty with the imprecatory Psalms and believe they are inappropriate for recitation by those who have Jesus and the love command at the heart of their faith. The rejection of a part of Scripture may indicate an unwillingness to deal with the reality of rage and vindictiveness which lies deep within our psyche. At a conference I attended a few years ago the person leading morning prayer excised several verses from the Psalms because they came into this category. We then continued reciting the verses at a point where the Psalmist was being incredibly smug about his own goodness and the fact that God was on his side! It seems that anger was to be suppressed in a Christian context, but it was acceptable to adopt a stance of self-righteous superiority.

God loves me and Jesus tells me to love my enemies and pray for those who persecute me. But it is a struggle to arrive at the place where I can actually do what he says because first I have to deal with the sense of injury and injustice which makes the loving so difficult. I *do* feel rage, I *do* want God to take vengeance on my attacker, and I would be happy to see those who misunderstand and reject me destroyed. The temptation may be to suppress and reject such feelings. After all, I "ought" to be a loving, forgiving person; I "ought" to recognize my own destructiveness and the hurt I have caused others. But at this moment, I do not, and unless I express what is really in my heart, inviting God to share it and to experience me at my worst, I am not praying with honesty. The imprecatory Psalms have a therapeutic quality to them because in the expression of howling rage I am led to new perspectives of how things actually are and the assurance that God has not abandoned me because I did not meet my own standards of Christian perfection.

Psalm 55 offers one example of the healing potential in a genuine expression of anguish and the desire for revenge. It begins with a cry to God to listen and understand what is happening to the pray-er:

> Hear my prayer, O God;
> do not hide yourself from my petition!
> Listen to me and answer me;
> I have no peace because of my cares.
> I am shaken by the noise of the enemy
> and by the pressure of the wicked . . . .
> Fear and trembling have come over me;
> and horror overwhelms me.

The sense of oppression is so great that the Psalmist longs to escape, to run away from the reality of the present moment:

> And I said, "Oh, that I had wings like a dove!
> I would fly away and be at rest."

But this is no answer; it is simply a refusal to deal with what actually is. So instead, there follows an expression of the vindictiveness which is being felt:

> Swallow them up, O Lord;
> confound their speech . . . .
> Let death come upon them suddenly;
> let them go down alive into the grave . . . .

Reading between the lines we learn that it is not so much the hostility of "them" as the personal betrayal by a close friend which has caused the Psalmist such deep pain:

> My companion stretched forth his hand
> against his comrade;
> He has broken his covenant.

This was a "familiar" friend about whom the writer could say:

> We took sweet counsel together,
> and walked with the throng in the house of God.

Trust has been broken, leaving the Psalmist bereft of the intimacy and support on which he relied. In the expression of his anger and feeling of aloneness, he realizes that God is the one unshakable foundation and source of hope, and he counsels himself:

> Cast your burden upon the Lord,
> and he will sustain you . . . .

The focus of attention has moved from the instability of human relationships to trust in God as sustainer and burden bearer. Hope is reborn and the future seems possible.

But the Psalms are not fairy tales with "happy ever after" endings. Even in the closing verses, the Psalmist entertains thoughts of vindication which will include the destruction of those who oppose him:

> For you will bring the bloodthirsty and deceitful
> down to the pit of destruction, O God.
> They shall not live out half their days,
> but I will put my trust in you.

This reminds us that our attempts at forgiveness of those who hurt us are often far from complete and may need to be made again and again. Sometimes all I can do is express my vindictiveness and desire for revenge, letting God hear this as my prayer, and then consent to wait until forgiveness is possible. With really deep wounds healing may take a long time, but waiting for the capacity to forgive, living with the injury and my feeling about the one who caused it, is far more authentic than suppressing the reality. And God honors authentic prayer.

One of the results of facing the way things are is a growing awareness of our own brokenness and need for forgiveness. It is at these times that the Psalms of penitence provide us with a way of praying. The best known of the penitential Psalms is 51, traditionally linked with David's repentance following his adultery with Bathsheba, and responsibility for her husband's death. It is, of course, associated with the liturgy of Ash Wednesday and Good Friday for many Christians.

> Have mercy on me, O God, according
> to your loving-kindness;
> in your great compassion blot out my offenses.
> Wash me through and through from my wickedness...
> For I know my transgressions,
> and my sin is ever before me.

19

Deep, unabsolved guilt overwhelms the Psalmist, and he cannot forget his offense. However, he does not opt for the destructive way of forgetting and self-justification. Instead, he tells it as it really is; he takes responsibility for his sin and owns the painful reality of it to the Lord. He looks for a way to begin again, a renewal of his being which only God can effect:

> Create in me a clean heart, O God,
> and renew a right spirit within me.
> Cast me not away from your presence
> and take not your Holy Spirit from me.
> Give me the joy of your saving help again
> and sustain me with your bountiful Spirit.

Here we meet a person living with the painful reality of who he is, and allowing that to be expressed as prayer. We constantly experience ourselves as frail, inadequate, sinful—though we may prefer psychological jargon to express our human condition. There comes a moment, however, when owning what we are is of far greater importance than explaining it. We need forgiveness, not psychological readjustment or a redefining of our moral and ethical base. And the healing begins in the honest confession to our Creator of those things and attitudes which prevent us living the faith we proclaim. The guilt which the Psalmist feels and expresses is entirely appropriate, and so too is his way of dealing with it. He does not choose to appease God by engaging in diversionary activity:

> Had you desired it, I would have offered sacrifice,
> but you take no delight in burnt-offerings.
> The sacrifice of God is a troubled spirit;
> a broken and contrite heart, O God, you will not
> despise.

The sin is real; the guilt is real; confession leads to forgiveness, as the attempt to salve conscience by making atonement through religious duty could not.

Issues of guilt and atonement are very complex and psychology can help a great deal in the identification of inappropriate guilt feelings and attempts to dispel them. My own experience in therapy has taught me a great deal about the way in which past experience, and especially the formative first years of life, condition my present responses. Human growth takes place as I become aware of these things and free myself from their grip by refusing the false guilt which accrues from them. But I make a mistake if I think I can ever find total healing through this process, because I need also to take responsibility for who I am and the way I respond to life. This will sometimes mean owning my deepest failures as the sin which they are, and coming penitently to the God who loves and accepts me. Penitence and thanksgiving find powerful expression in Psalm 103:

> Bless the Lord, O my soul,
> and all that is within me, bless his holy Name.
> Bless the Lord, O my soul,
> and forget not all his benefits.
> He forgives all your sins
> and heals all your infirmities . . . .

The forgiveness and healing experienced following confession leads the Psalmist to express gratitude and worship. Another substantial category of Psalmody is thanksgiving and the note of celebration and joy sounds constantly. Many of these Psalms were written to celebrate some great historical event of God's saving activity, such as the Exodus from Egypt. The restoration of the people of Israel is celebrated in Ps. 126, and the annual Autumn Festival, culminating in the enthronement ceremony in the Temple where the crowning of the Davidic king symbolized Yahweh's epiphany, is the subject of many Psalms. Others rejoice at God's forgiveness, healing, answers to prayer, creative activity, care for the people, and presence in the midst of life. Often the singing of these Psalms was accompanied by dance and a variety of musical instruments (Ps. 150).

Thanking God was paramount in Hebrew worship and this was not a perfunctory grace before meals, or a sentence in the weekly liturgy, but an activity which engaged the whole person. Body, mind and spirit together rejoiced at Yahweh's goodness, celebrating with joy the presence of the living God in the midst of the people. Psalm 138 offers one example of this:

> I will give thanks to you, O Lord, with my whole heart;
> before the gods will I sing your praise.
> I will bow down toward your holy temple and praise your
> name.
> because of your love and faithfulness....
> When I called, you answered me;
> you increased my strength within me....
> Though the Lord be high, he cares for the lowly....

and Psalm 149 says:

> Hallelujah!
> Sing to the Lord a new song
> sing his praise in the congregation of the faithful
> Let Israel rejoice in his maker;
> Let the children of Zion be joyful in their King.
> Let them praise his Name in the dance;
> Let them sing praise to him with timbrel and harp.

How much Western Christians, whose worship is so often cerebral and constrained, need to rediscover this dimension of prayer! Dance is one of the most powerful ways to pray the Psalms. Today Liturgical Dance is less uncommon than it was a few years ago, but there are still many congregations who have never experienced this kind of creative worship. Some would even question the validity of dance in the context of worship. In 1978 I was leading an Easter Mission in Wales, with a group of seminarians, and on the evening of Easter Day we celebrated with dance and a variety of musical instruments. Members of the congregation, together with those of us who were visiting, had worked to create this celebration of the risen Christ. We had studied, discussed and above all, danced our way into the text, not to offer a performance but to present our whole bodies "as a living sacrifice holy and acceptable to God." Nevertheless, when the dance began one lady left, snorting with indignation, that she had lived to see the day when there was "dancing in the Lord's house"! She failed totally to understand that this was precisely where God's people danced the Psalms she so loved to recite at morning and evening prayer—and they did not confine themselves to a pipe organ for accompaniment!

The liberating power of dance and bodily movement cannot be overstressed, for it has the capacity to put us in touch with the deep parts of ourselves which are often neglected. It takes us beyond words, indeed indicates the inadequacy of words alone to express our innermost longings, fears, hopes and joys. Self-consciousness is soon lost when a group of people realize that dance-prayer is not a show, but a profound expression of their own desire to pray in new ways. Once at a workshop in a Roman Catholic convent in England we spent an entire weekend creating dance to offer as our expression of prayer at the final Eucharist we were to share together. The movement evolved naturally as we immersed ourselves in the Scriptures for the day, particularly the appointed Psalms. My most vivid memory from that weekend is of the eighty-year-old sister who took to her heels as soon as the Mass ended, and with tambourine led us in a long, snake-like song and dance to the Refectory. This was an unscheduled piece of joy in which she celebrated her release from long years of conditioning which suggested that stillness and solemnity alone were appropriate prayer postures.

The Psalms can also be danced in the privacy of one's own room and as part of our personal prayers. Reading the Psalm thoughtfully, asking "How does this made me feel?" may be a way into using the body to pray. Sometimes music will form a useful stimulus; a Bach cantata for some of the gentle, meditative Psalms or Holst's "Planets Suite" to provide a background for those expressing anger. But the important thing is to listen to the Scripture and listen to one's own body response. As we learn to respect our bodies and to free ourselves from the unconscious dualism which suggests they are less worthy than our minds, we will be able to pray in a more integrated fashion to the God in whose image we are created, and who sanctified our humanity by becoming flesh and dwelling among us!

A further category of Psalms focuses on the expression of anguish and, sometimes, despair. The best known of the Psalms of lament is 137. The people of Israel are exiled in Babylon and far from home and the temple on Mount Zion, the center of their worship and faith. They bewail their lot:

> By the waters of Babylon we sat down and wept,
> when we remembered you, O Zion.
> As for our harps, we hung them up
> on the trees in the midst of that land.
> For those who led us away captive asked us for a song,
> and our oppressors called for mirth:
> "Sing us one of the songs of Zion."
> How shall we sing the Lord's song upon an alien soil?

Their prayer at this point is an expression of grief, of the loss of roots, and a lamenting over their present suffering. To pretend to a joy they were not experiencing would have been inauthentic and so they simply poured out their sadness at the way things were.

There are times when lament becomes little more than an expression of self-pity. If the pray-er gets stuck in all the negativity by which he or she is surrounded and goes on reciting the same old problems ad infinitum, the only result is to be confirmed in the belief that life is basically bad. But there is a healthy kind of lamentation, and the expression of grief to God is a necessary part of prayer if we are to find healing. Sometimes life is unfair; tragic things happen and there is no one to blame for them, but we need to pray through our grief and loss. Sharing the grieving process with God then becomes our prayer. We may find ourselves blaming God for not making things turn out differently (and it is no use telling ourselves that intellectually we do not believe in that kind of "magician" God anyway). We want someone to blame and our rational convictions may not prove very helpful in the light of our emotional reactions, so blaming God may be the best thing we can do at the moment. After all, God can handle the accusations far better than those who may later be the recipients of them because such reactions have been suppressed. And God will go on loving us come what may. Psalm 88 at times moves from genuine lament into wheedling self-pity, and ends on a note of hopeless gloom:

> O Lord, my God, my Savior,
> by day and night I cry to you.
> Let my prayer enter into your presence;
> incline your ear to my lamentation . . . .
> My sight has failed me because of trouble;
> Lord, I have called upon you daily,
> I have stretched out my hands to you . . . .
> Lord, why have you rejected me?
> why have you hidden your face from me?
> Ever since my youth, I have been wretched and at the
>   point of death;
> I have borne your terrors with a troubled mind . . . .
> My friend and my neighbor you have put away from me,
> and darkness is my only companion.

There is more than a hint of paranoia in the latter part of this Psalm, and that suggests that the Psalmist's perceptions are not very accurate. Perhaps we may recognize ourselves here, too.

The underlying conviction of the Scripture is that God is, and that God is good, and so is all that God has made. But the experience of life quickly teaches us to doubt the reality of God, and seriously to question that goodness, God's or anyone else's, is fundamental. We come up against so much badness in ourselves and others, and so much uncontrolled suffering, that all we can do is groan with anguish. At the end of our lamenting we may begin to catch a glimpse of hope and of some more data which will help us redefine our present pain. We may even be given the grace to laugh at ourselves a little. But in the meantime this is where we are, stuck with our grief, and honestly pouring it out to the God who has failed to meet our expectations.

When Jesus cried out on the cross, "My God, my God, why have you forsaken me?" he was lamenting in the words of the Psalter that the pain was excruciating, and that he felt utterly abandoned. At that point it would not have been helpful if some post-Chalcedonian Christian had come along and told him all would be well because resurrection was just around the corner. Nor would he have been supported by one of his fellow countrymen telling him God never abandoned the just and he would be posthumously vindicated. What he was experiencing was the "real absence" of God and so with simple candor he asked the question. "Why, God? Why now of all times do you choose to desert me?" This is not self-pity. In fact, throughout the Passion Jesus is revealed facing pain, expressing his desire to resist it, but consenting to be attentive to it in a genuinely caring way. The Psalter helps him pray in reality, to ask the crucial questions, and to be present to all the dark horror of that moment.

There is a Pollyanna-ish kind of approach to prayer which is not really authentic because it fails to deal with the reality of suffering. The Bible affirms that God loves and cares for us through the joys and pains of life, but it also allows us to be real about the devastating power of adversity. It invites us, especially through the Psalter, to express our doubts, fear, need, blame, anger, and even to accuse God of infidelity. As we take the route to genuine prayer, we are led deeper into faith, and our vision of ourselves, God, and the world is broadened. There is hope in spite of it all, but it is not hope centered in a fantasy world devoid of real pain. It is the assurance that "all shall be well," as Julian of Norwich told us, but we can only say that when, like her, we accept the painful contradictions of life and consent to live them.

One of my favorite biblical Psalms is found at the end of the prophecy of Habakkuk. Things are not good for the prophet, and he does not pretend that they are, yet he proclaims faith in the God of joy who enables him to penetrate the gloom and even to dance—one translator has "spin around with delight"—in the God of his salvation. This is real faith, because it is not dependent on things getting better, but on finding God in the midst of adverse circumstances:

Though the fig tree do not blossom,
nor fruit be on the vines,
the produce of the olive fail
and the fields yield no food,
the flock be cut off from the fold
and there be no herd in the stalls,
yet I will rejoice in the Lord,
I will joy in the God of my salvation.
God, the Lord, is my strength;
he makes my feet like hinds' feet,
he makes me tread upon my high places.

KNOWING THE SCRIPTURES

My delight is in your statutes;
I will not forget your word. (Ps. 119:16)

The Psalmist's delight in the Scriptures sprang from a thorough acquaintance with them and a sense of identity within the community that gave them birth. These writings were the lifeblood of Hebrew culture, determining appropriate behavior and relationships and undergirding the holy worship of a transcendent God. In many ways our easy access to books has disadvantaged us. The capacity to remember, retain and reflect on the Bible (or any other ancient literature) is far less developed in our Western culture. Despite the availability of commentaries and study aids, the average Christian knows comparatively little of the content of the Bible. Living in a mobile, pluralistic society also diminishes our sense of community and so the tribal identity of the Hebrews is strange to us. We are faced with the problem of how to know, digest and pray the Scriptures in a meaningful way. Learning to pray the Psalms is a good starting point, but what of the rest of the Bible? This collection of history, saga, poetry, law, liturgy, myth, letters and gospels, written over several centuries, is baffling to say the least. Some of it is downright boring; many of its presuppositions are abhorrent to us, the condoning of genocide, racial and sexual oppression, religious intolerance, and it bears little relation to any other literature with which we are familiar.

People cannot pray the Bible if they do not know it, or if they have tried to read it but found it incomprehensible. When the German theologian Rudolf Bultmann was preaching to the troops in the Second World War and realized that his ministry failed because they could not grasp the relevance of the Bible, he came to see that another way of interpreting the Scripture was

29

necessary. He was not simply setting a new trend in theology, but acting out of an existential need. He suggested that the Bible needed to be "demythologized," that is, the essence of its teaching had to be set free from the thought forms of the time when it was written. His radical analysis, which proved to be threatening to many conservatives, set his hearers free to encounter the Word in their own experience.

In Bultmann's terms myth is a primitive, pre-scientific conceptualization of reality and as such it does not comprehend the true causes of natural or mental processes. Since the Bible represents the other world in terms which are spatial and material, since it assumes the three tiered universe described in the last chapter, since it attributes mental disorders to demons and assumes the existence of spiritual powers causing events in the world, it can be spoken of as mythological. For example, the Parousia, the return of Christ on the clouds, is not a literal but a mythical expression of the truth that he comes and will come to set humanity free. His victory over demons is a means of proclaiming his healing power and purpose to make people whole. In other words, Bultmann suggests that we cannot simply cling to a first-century world view because that would mean accepting in our religious thinking a position we deny in our everyday life. It would set up a conflict which might well result in a relegation of religion to the dustpile of the obsolete. Instead he invites us to demythologize the Scriptures. We do not have to discard the myth, for it represents truth inexpressible in other forms, but we do have to interpret it in our own context.

In many ways this was what we were doing in the the last chapter as we allowed the Psalms to become vehicles for prayer, even though some of their imagery is obscure to us. Similarly, liberation theology takes an existential perspective to enable people to make their own connections with the text. The rigorous academic scrutiny of Bultmann and his successors may be lacking, but the Word lives in and for the peasant farmers and their families who have ears to hear. This is not to suggest that continued critical research is unnecessary. It will always be important to have the professional theologians engaging in the task of exegesis and making their findings available to the wider church. But the Scriptures are for us all.

The last chapter largely addressed the question of personal prayer, and ways in which we can use the Psalter to express our joy, pain, grief, yearning and fear. It is also enriching to pray the Bible in the context of a group, and a number of ways to do this are open to us. Three models for group study and prayer are offered in this chapter and it concludes with a comment on the value of journal writing as a means of integrating the insights gained.

MODEL I:

Imagination is a wonderful gift which enables us to enter worlds full of mystery, adventure, and magic. To watch children at play is to be reminded of the fairy tale world of our own early imaginings, when anything seemed possible. We have moved on from dragons, castles, kingdoms and princes that inhabited the fantasies of our childhood, becoming wiser, less spontaneous and perhaps a trifle cynical about such delight in "let's pretend." But the truth is we still do a good deal of fantasizing about life. What if. . . I won the lottery. . . lost my job. . . married X or Y. . . became famous. . . such thoughts can occupy us for hours and help to relieve the tedium of the present. We can, of course, become escapists always in flight from the present moment, but our capacity for imagination can also be harnessed to enliven things for us. This is especially true of the Scriptures.

The gospels in particular take on new depths of meaning when we use our power of imagination to enter into their story and identify with the individuals the writer brings before us. This kind of approach to the gospels may be used in a group setting where a leader sets the scene and guides our thinking. It is equally valuable as an individual exercise.

It is important to begin by relaxing the body, and setting the mind free of the many distractions that demand attention. This takes time, but it helps if the eyes are closed and the breathing deep and regular. The repetition of a mantra or use of prayer beads may also help in the slowing down, centering process. When the group is ready, read slowly the passage of Scripture chosen for the exercise and at the end allow a few moments of silence. Then begin to enter the world of your imagination as you place yourself in the scene and become the various characters in the story. The following two examples of the method come directly from my own experience. In the first I was a participant in a group exercise, and the second is an account of my own imaginative work with the gospel reading in the regular daily lectionary. The group experience is recorded as though the leader is speaking throughout, and is based on the well-known story of the Good Samaritan. Obviously, time was allowed between each statement for the participants to imagine the scene and react to the story.

The scene is Jerusalem. Take time to look around you. Be aware of the buildings, the people, animals. Notice the colors and textures of things. What kind of sounds do you hear? Are you aware of any smell, fragrance or odor? What kind of day is this? You are about to set out on a journey leaving Jerusalem, set high in the Judean hills, to descend down into the Jordan Valley to Jericho. You know that this route is not very safe for lone travelers. How do you feel as you set out? As you get further away from the city, look back and see the place you have left behind. What are your feelings about it now? Now look ahead. Notice the hills resting on each side of the roadway which leads steadily down. How does this wilderness area look? Is there any plant or animal life? Any people on the road? What time of day is it? Be aware of your feelings as you continue walking downwards.

Suddenly, without warning, robbers appear and they attack you. What do they look like? What do they do to you? After they have beaten you they leave; how do you feel now, left alone and badly injured beside the road? Be aware of the physical discomfort. What passes through your mind as you lie there? Time passes. Then in the distance you hear footsteps approaching. What do you feel as they draw nearer? What do you do? When the person is close enough you see that he is a priest, a highly respected religious leader. What are your feelings now? He reaches you and walks by on the other side of the roadway. What does this make you feel and do? Again you are alone. Be aware of what is happening to your body and in your mind. After another long time has elapsed more footsteps are heard. What do you think and feel this time? As the other person gets nearer what do you do? When he is close enough to be recognized as a Levite, yet another honored leader of Temple worship, how do you feel? What happens in you when he also passes you by, even though he has seen your condition? Be aware of your feelings as you are once again alone with your injuries.

When you hear footsteps for a third time, how do you react? Notice your feelings as the person draws near. How do you respond when you realize that this man is a Samaritan, a member of that radical, schismatic group despised by the orthodox? As he comes near to you what do you expect will happen? What do you think and feel as he stoops down to where you are lying and begins to tend your wounds? Be aware of the way he touches you and see the compassion in his eyes. What are your feelings as this stranger expresses his care for you? What do you do and say to him? Now he is helping you onto his donkey and together you continue the journey downwards until you come to an inn. The Samaritan helps you dismount, and settles you into a safe and comfortable place. What are your feelings towards him now? As he leaves he not only pays for your lodging but tells the innkeeper he will take care of all future expenses until you are well. Be aware of your body. Of the thoughts that pass through your mind, and of what you say to the Samaritan. Then in your own time, when you are ready, leave the world of your imagination, open your eyes and once again become aware of this time and place.

On the occasion when I was a participant in this exercise we then shared verbally what the experience had meant to us, and the issues that had become clear as we experienced it. Some people were angry with the church, symbolized by its two representatives who ignored the injured man, and they recalled some of their own hurts which needed healing. Others were in touch with times in their own lives when they had felt violated and alone, almost giving up hope of finding help. Another person was aware of feelings of guilt for times when he had closed his eyes to some obvious need because action would be inconvenient or damaging. For others the risk of the human journey was paramount, especially when the choice of direction leads to a lonely path.

In discussing these various reactions to the story, it becomes clear how we are to pray. It may be that we need to forgive the church or God for the times when we have felt ourselves neglected or ignored. That prayer will almost certainly involve us in a commitment to reach out to others who may be feeling that way, and to make their community a more caring and hospitable place. The awareness of our own sense of violation may lead to the expression of anger which is healing, and even to a recognition of some of our own inner violence and vindictiveness. Some of the guilt about lost opportunities to minister to those in need is fully appropriate, and brings us to penitence and a commitment to be present to the need of others in the future. If we stand poised on the brink of some new adventure, some new risk that may isolate us from the companionship of others, then our prayer will be for courage to take the necessary steps forward.

Although on this occasion we did not go on to do this, it would be instructive to tell the story again, placing ourselves in the role of the Samaritan. As one despised by the Jewish population, marginalized by society, used to hostile looks and actions, how did he feel about this journey? What was his initial reaction to the injured man? What motivated him to act with compassion? We could thus become aware of our own sense of alienation and how we react to it, and also conscious of that complex mixture of fear, anger, revenge, hope, love and caring which makes up our personality. Equally we could place ourselves in the shoes of the priest or Levite, though I suspect we might want to resist identifying ourselves with the "bad guys," and allow into consciousness the methods of self protection we employ. We would begin to see our unwillingness to be involved in situations that we think will be costly, especially if our public image is at stake. We could begin to pray through some of our superficiality and hypocrisy as we learn again that the heart of religion is

> to do justice, and to love kindness,
> and to walk humbly with your God. (Mic. 6.8)

MODEL II:

Some months ago the daily lectionary readings were from St. Luke's gospel and I found the story in 7:36-50 occupied me for several mornings as I worked imaginatively with it.

One of the Pharisees asked him to eat with him, and
he went into the Pharisee's house, and took his place
at table. And behold, a woman of the city, who
was a sinner, when she learned that he was at
table in the Pharisee's house, brought an alabaster
flask of ointment, and standing behind him at his
feet, weeping, she began to wet his feet with her
tears, and wiped them with the hair of her head, and
kissed his feet, and anointed them with ointment.
Now when the Pharisee who had invited him saw it,
he said to himself, "If this man were a prophet, he
would have known who and what sort of woman this
is who is touching him, for she is a sinner." And Jesus
answering said to him, "Simon, I have something to
say to you." And he answered, "What is it, Teacher?"
"A certain creditor had two debtors: one owed five
hundred denarii, and the other fifty. When they could
not pay, he forgave them both. Now which of them
will love him more?" Simon answered, "The one, I
suppose, to whom he forgave more." And he said to
him, "You have judged rightly." Then turning toward
the woman he said to Simon, "Do you see this
woman? I entered your house, you gave me no water
for my feet, but she has wet my feet with her tears
and wiped them with her hair. You gave me no kiss,
but from the time I came in she has not ceased to
kiss my feet. You did not anoint my head with oil,
but she has anointed my feet with ointment.
Therefore I tell you, her sins, which are many, are
forgiven, for she loved much; but he who is forgiven
little, loves little." And he said to her, "Your sins are
forgiven." Then those who were at table with him
began to say among themselves, "Who is this, who
even forgives sins?" And he said to the woman,
"Your faith has saved you; go in peace."

I began by recalling the context in which Luke places the
event. Immediately before Jesus received the invitation to dinner
at the home of a Pharisee he had been dealing with a "no win"
situation. The impact of his ministry was shocking, and disturbed
traditional thinking and social custom. He broke the rules by ap-

pealing to a higher law, that of compassion for every person, and by so doing made the leaders of his people uncomfortable. They were out to get him, and the Pharisees in particular are singled out as his critics.[1] John the Baptist was criticized because he was too ascetical, too committed to self-denial and fasting. Jesus, on the other hand, enjoyed parties and accepted gratefully the hospitality of others, so they called him a glutton and a drunkard, a friend of tax collectors and sinners. This was a generation that Jesus compared to children sitting in the market place, quarrelling because no one wanted to join in their games. They were dissatisfied, complaining irritably to one another because their expectations were not fulfilled, but they had not identified what it was they actually wanted. And Jesus says, "Yet wisdom is justified by all her children." The New Testament writers made use of the feminine figure of Wisdom in the Hebrew Scriptures to speak of Jesus, sometimes explicitly and more often by implication.[2] Here Jesus seems to be implying that those who recognize him for who he is, and respond as children to a loving parent, are all the justification he requires. He does not need to be tossed about by the expectations and criticisms of others, as long as he lives by fidelity to his own inner wisdom. This is important contextual material which throws light on the story which follows and suggests some ways to understand the responses of the three major characters in the drama.

I began by visualizing the Pharisee who was Jesus' host, imagining his appearance, the design of his home and the table set for a meal. I tried to guess why he had invited Jesus. It did not appear to me that this was simply a hostile attempt to entrap the Lord. The Pharisee seemed genuinely disappointed when Jesus demonstrated that he was not a real prophet, since he did not recognize the woman's sinfulness. At the same time neglect of normal courtesies, such as offering his guest water to wash the dust of the road from his feet, suggested to me that Simon was half-hearted in his reception of Jesus. Perhaps he felt embarrassed by what his respectable friends would think about his hosting of the itinerant rabbi whose credentials were so suspect. I began to be aware of the mixture of motives out of which this man acted, the genuine desire to know as well as the fear and hypocrisy that prevented a real openness to the compassion of Jesus. I found myself enjoying his discomfort as Jesus exposed the shallowness of his thinking, and like the Psalmist I rejoiced over the downfall of this enemy. The feelings of vindictiveness were strong!

At this point I thought it was important to look at what was happening in me as I reflected on the character of Simon, the Pharisee—what was going on at a subconscious level that caused such a strong reaction? I had seen that his motivations were very mixed and had been able to recognize that I too respond to truth from "good" and "bad" motives, so why was I so glad to see him put down? It was then that I realized an old wound was being opened, for Simon represented the institution, the tradition, orthodoxy. I had unconsciously made a leap from first-century Judaism to the twentieth-century Christian church! As a woman, in what is still largely a patriarchal institution, I have often felt marginalized by the power structure and the hierarchy. As a priest I often feel "on trial," for the visibility of women in holy orders continues to evoke strong emotions, especially in those for whom this is a new experience. In order to be ordained I had to leave the branch of the Anglican Communion in which I found my roots because it was still not ready to test the vocation of women to the priesthood. So Simon became those intransigent, frightened, chauvinistic clergy who persisted in forcing a "no" vote in the Church of England. No wonder I was glad to see him humiliated! In this story the tables are turned; the mighty are put down from their seats and the lowly are raised up!

This is not, of course, a rational response to the story, and it illustrates how readily our unconscious presuppositions distort the text for us, but it does constitute an invitation to prayer. The feelings generated were real, and needed to be acknowledged and accepted for what they were. The hostile, angry part of ourselves, which is ready to apportion blame to an amorphous "them," is the part of us which now prays. In the articulation of my reaction to Simon came fresh insight too. Perspective was distorted by past experience but that does not mean that it was entirely wrong. There are attitudes and structures in today's church which need to be challenged and changed. It seems that, whether I want it or not, I am often cast in the role of catalyst, and the acceptance of that vocation is an ongoing process. So now the prayer becomes a fresh "yes" to God, which includes the willingness to allow the oppressor to be seen in a new light, and to pray for him too.

The next stage of this imaginative working with the story was to place myself in Jesus' dusty sandals. Already I was beginning to identify with him as marginalized and on trial, with perhaps a hint of paranoia creeping into my thinking. At the outset he accepted Simon's invitation and seemed ready to be present to his host, accepting him for who he was rather than prejudging his integrity. Then the meal was interrupted by a needy woman of doubtful reputation who lavished an embarrassing overflow of love on Jesus. At this point I felt very in touch with how often I feel divided by the conflicting needs of people. It is all too easy to use an opportunity to win over those who question my credibility, and to ignore the loving attention of others. In what evolves in the story, I see that Jesus does not take responsibility for the feelings of other people, but he does help them to recognize what is going on within.

The next stage is to address the Pharisee unspoken question, not shrinking from honesty, though it may cost him the approval of this man. Why is Jesus allowing this outrage? Why doesn't he realize what kind of a woman this is and keep himself pure from contact? Jesus involves Simon in the parable in a way which would cause great discomfort, but make the issues clear. At the same time he validates the woman's generosity of spirit and touches the real issue for her, confidently pronouncing God's forgiveness and offering her peace. The inner wisdom of Jesus and his centeredness make him truly present to those who encounter him. He does not need the masks of superiority, power or external credentials, for he has a deep self-assurance. I find myself praying to become more like him; less dependent on the approval of others, more in touch with my own wisdom, more secure in fulfilling my own vocation. In my journal I wrote:

> Living Christ, give me the wisdom to know what is
> true, the courage to act upon it, and the confidence
> to share your healing power. Amen.

Finally I turned to the woman who came with such audacity and passionate longing to the feet of Jesus. Why did she come? She must have met or heard of Jesus previously to want to lavish such extravagance on him. St. Luke specializes in stories about those who were without rights, pushed to the edge of society; children, lepers, Samaritans, women. She would seem to be one of those in this category who found in Jesus someone who revealed her own worth to her and opened up the possibility of new life. How did she get into the house? Surely servants and other guests would have recognized her and tried to prevent one known as a prostitute from entering, and therefore rendering others "unclean" by her presence. The fact that she was there suggested she was a woman of great determination and courage in whom Jesus stirred generosity of spirit. I wonder about the embarrassment of Simon and Jesus at her entry, but even more at her overcoming the fear that she would be humiliated. She must have known that she was walking right into a hostile context where she would experience criticism, rejection and probably expulsion, but she took the risk. Not only were her morals questionable, but to advance to the table where only men were seated challenged the sexual taboos of the day.

I am impressed by the temerity of this woman and aware of times when I have risked myself. In my prayer I celebrate those moments which have represented the overcoming of fear and reticence, and have become occasions of trust. I recognize that we perceive Jesus in different ways which satisfy our own deep needs and myths, but the yearning for all he embodies is like a drug. And suddenly I have the shocking image of Jesus as the insect-trap! The insects are inexorably drawn to its light and there consumed by its power. I realize how limited this is as a symbol of who Christ is for us, but it did come to mind and so must have some truth for me. However much I resist, try to turn away, or look in a different direction I am drawn back to that consuming, burning love. And through the death of the little frightened ego with which I protect myself, a new life is born, resurrection takes place.

I ended my journal entry with these words:

You have made us for yourself and our hearts
are restless till they find their rest in you.
(Augustine)

I hunger and I thirst,
Jesus my manna be
Ye living waters burst
out of the rock for me.

She comes with her love and with her need for healing and she pours it out over the feet of Jesus. She stays as the questioning takes place, and she hears the words of reassurance and absolution. She can go

in peace because she has received from the Lord the
gift of herself.

Praise, my soul, the King of Heaven;
To his feet thy tribute bring;
Ransomed, healed, restored, forgiven,
Evermore his praises sing:
Alleluia! Alleluia!
Praise the everlasting king.

The kind of group exercise I described earlier is very rewarding, for we learn a good deal from each other's insights into
the Scriptures. Many people, however, are denied the possibility
of that kind of meeting whether because of geography, age, or
family commitment. The second approach can be used in a
group, but it is available to individuals and opens up the gospels
in new, exciting ways. To begin with, some people may experience a little difficulty in using the imagination to enter the stories, but it is worth persisting with the method. In time we learn
to trust the sometimes neglected gift of imagination, and to set
aside our fears of not "getting it right." The Scriptures are the
Word of God and this is one of the ways in which we can begin
to converse with them and integrate the good news into our
own experience.

Introducing others to the joy of biblical prayer is best accomplished by an enthusiastic teacher, one who is excited by the
intrinsic relevance of the Scriptures. Nothing communicates
more powerfully than a living witness to the contemporary, life-
affirming Word of God, as the experience of the post-Pentecost
disciples makes clear. Although it is helpful if a group leader has
done some prior work on the text to be considered, of far
greater importance is an attitude of openness, honesty and the
recognition that we are all artists/students discovering new pat-
terns day by day. The leader's role does not consist of filling
people with more information, but rather in facilitating the

sharing of insight. The invitation to search the Scriptures and offer personal responses in an atmosphere of trust sets people free from dependence on the professional authority figures. It also leads to a search for deeper understanding, inspired not by a guilty feeling that they "ought" to know more, but by an excitement about what they have discovered already.

MODEL III:

An approach that I have found useful with many different groups involves the selection of a passage of Scripture, which is first read in silence by each participant. Ten to twelve verses are usually selected for this purpose. Time is allowed for personal reflection, and at that point some people prefer to write down their thoughts. I ask them to consider how the passage in question relates to their own lives, and suggest a first quick reading followed by a more reflective verse by verse consideration of it. Then the group is divided into pairs, and each person is invited to share with one other any thoughts that have emerged about the passage. It is far less threatening to talk with one other person about personal responses to the text than to speak them to a large group, and even the most shy person present will have something to say. After adequate time has been allowed for this dialogue—the leader will need to exercise discernment about the appropriate period, but usually ten to fifteen minutes is adequate—the group is reconvened. At this point anyone who chooses to do so may offer their reflections, and discussion follows as the group responds. I am often surprised by the profound insights which come from those who initially declared themselves ignorant of the Bible and incompetent as interpreters. The confidence gained by talking to one person enables them to trust their own understanding, and they feel affirmed as others make connections with it.

The kind of discussion which develops from this method is far more wide ranging than is usually the case with Model II. Often the focus of the group will be centered on issues far removed from the passage, though originating in it. We are not trying to "be" the characters, to place ourselves in someone else's shoes, but to allow the story to generate thoughts and ideas for us. While this dialogue is going on the leader listens, encourages, and sometimes elucidates the comments. Sometimes it will be necessary to help participants clarify what they are saying, or to move their thinking a stage further by introducing a question. However this is never done in a way that suggests that the speaker is mistaken or that the thoughts offered to the group are inadequate. The emphasis is always on valuing what has been said and allowing it to become a vehicle for further discussion. Members of the group can also respond to each other. At times a specific question relating to the background of the passage will emerge, and this is where the leader's prior study will be helpful. For example, in the story of Simon the Pharisee and the woman who anointed Jesus, it is informative to know something about the food laws and social taboos which were enforced at the time. This will throw into even sharper relief the refusal of Jesus to be conditioned by the prevailing culture, and may well open up a discussion of our own connivance with prevailing hypocrisy. Such background knowledge will also prove invaluable in the final gathering together of themes and reflections, but it is not undertaken in order to impose an academic lecture to validate the exercise. Often people will ask for elucidation on biblical customs, the original meaning of certain images or figures of speech, where an event took place, or why a particular statement was made. In all good teaching, interest is elicited by involving the students in the educative process, and this Bible study method aims at precisely that. First the text touches their lives, then they experience a hunger to understand it more fully. This final summarizing by the leader is crucial, for in the process all participants can be affirmed in their own search and encouraged to pursue it further. Connection can also be made with other biblical passages which inform or connect with the one studied.

The last stage in this method is the identifying of prayer themes which emerge. For groups who are comfortable with extemporary prayer, a few specific topics might be mentioned before participants are invited to offer their own prayers. By a kind of free association, the prayers then follow in an unstructured form. For some this kind of praying will be strange, and instead a period of silence may follow in which each person makes her/his own meditation. Sometimes a visual symbol might be used as a focus for this. If, for example, the passage studied had been the Feeding of the Five Thousand, a loaf of bread might be used as a focus of meditation. Another possibility would be to invite group members to write their own prayers based on the themes of the study. This would be particularly relevant if some kind of liturgy was to follow, and would help those who feel nervous about praying aloud to overcome their reticence.

The discovery of the contemporaneity of the Bible through this group method often leads students to undertake serious courses of Scripture study because they want to be more fully informed about it. A further result is the desire to engage in personal study, and here, guidance will be needed. Many have found enthusiasm waning because they opted for the "logical" method of ploughing through the Bible from cover to cover. Most Christian denominations offer some form of daily Bible reading notes, and if the group leader is unfamiliar with such sources then local clergy may be able to help identify appropriate methods.

Those who come from the churches with a strong liturgical tradition might wish to use the daily lectionary readings as a basis for personal study. I have been surprised to discover how few members of the Episcopal Church have any idea how to use the Book of Common Prayer. I recently taught a Sunday morning adult Christian education course called the Liturgy of Lent. We took the set biblical texts and collects for the six Sundays of Lent, identified key themes, and discovered the interconnections between the various readings. A sense of excitement developed as we saw the relationship between different parts of Scripture and asked ourselves how we could take what we learned into our living of that season. When we began the course several participants did not know that they could turn to the back of the Book of Common Prayer and discover from the table of readings what Scriptures would be read in church. At least one parent determined to take time each week in the future to read and discuss them with the family as a preparation for entering more fully into Sunday worship.

JOURNALING WITH THE WORD

Writing in a prayer journal is a powerful way of making the connection between the written Word and its personal relevance. Writing down one's reflections on a Scripture passage is more than a simple recording of facts; it is a process. As the thoughts are written down new thoughts emerge and the writer enters into an inner dialogue. It is akin to the writing of a Gospel, because it is a way of expressing what the good news of God in Christ means to us. This is no second-hand story, but the Word of the living God spoken to and heard by us today. Sometimes a phrase will address us with such power we will read no further but savor it, ruminate upon it, allowing it to lodge deep in our consciousness. Our prayer will focus on this thought, and we can consciously take it with us into the day, maybe repeating it like a mantra during moments of quiet reflection.

All this sounds very encouraging and hopeful, but in reality I often do not experience reading the Scriptures in this way. Through my own tiredness, ill health, or just plain boredom with the routine of daily living and praying, I find that nothing has "spoken" to me that day. Emotionally I am unmoved and I have nothing to say to God. Alternatively, I might find myself irritated by the passage because it touches a sensitive nerve. I bring my past pain and prejudice to bear on the text and I want to reject it, eliminate it from the Scriptures. How do I pray the Bible in these circumstances? The temptation for any of us is to suppress these reactions because we have been taught to be nice people who always put on a good face for God. In other words, we have learned to make fig leaf aprons to mask the reality of who we really are as we hide in the garden of our deception. But this is not true prayer; I can only pray authentically from where I actually am, and if that happens to be on a flat, grey plain of boredom, then I had better learn to pray from there. What I have to offer God at that moment is my boredom, my lack of excitement with the Scriptures and so I consent to be where I am. I could, of course, go out and look for something new to excite me, for a religious shot to elevate me to a new high, but that would be to opt for unreality. In the same way my irritation or anger is an appropriate subject for prayer if that is what I am feeling. I may be very irrational and regressive in my response, but happily God loves that part of me too, though I often do not believe it.

It is at these times that a prayer journal is invaluable. Committing to writing the feeling and thoughts which come from this kind of reaction to the Scriptures enables us to process and, sometimes, to make sense of it and move on. It also helps us to bring before God what is really happening, and in the expression of our boredom and irritation, to find healing. The denial of what is really there is not only inauthentic, but may be destructive since it will eventually demand recognition. Then it may

HEARING THE WORD

His prayer was simply to realize the presence of God.[1]

We live in a culture which bombards us with words. They shout at us from billboards, newspapers, T.V. screens, computers; they drop into our mailbox every day; they circle the globe as we punch out numbers on a telephone and they come to us through books which inform, entertain and stimulate our search for knowledge. But we pay a price for progress. In the cacophony of voices clamoring to be heard we may be deaf to the word which gives life. Our attempts to listen become fragmented and our minds distracted by the sheer volume and variety of voices. How can we become focused and still enough to hear God's word, which addresses us in the midst of this exhilarating, but sometimes exhausting world of ours? How can we pray the Scriptures if we are unable to hear them? What can we do about distractions in prayer?

It is a comfort to know that distractions are a problem for the most experienced prayer as well as for the beginner. In fact distractedness is not something confined to our prayer; it is a symptom of the way we live our lives. Only occasionally do we really become attentive to what is going on at a particular moment, and wandering thoughts are common in most activities. As we get up in the morning our attention is not exclusively focused on the process of showering, dressing, and eating breakfast, but ranges over the numerous tasks and events which lie ahead. As we work our mind wanders to the show we will see that evening, the need to make a difficult telephone call. We do not pay attention to the dishes, letters, and people before us. It is not surprising, therefore, that we do not pay full attention to God when we take time for prayer. Knowing that distractions happen in other areas of our lives may help relieve some of the guilt associated with our failure to pay attention, but we also need to find a way through the chaos.

A simple but effective way to begin dealing with this problem is to identify the activities which really absorb us, and bring them into the orbit of our prayer. A very busy high school teacher, who is also the mother of four children and very active in her local parish, talked with me about her inability to concentrate when she prayed. Although she had practiced transcendental meditation for several years she found the voices of her job, children and leisure activities speaking more loudly than the voice of God in her prayer time. I asked her where, in her very full schedule, she experienced herself as most attentive. After a few moments' thought she said that working with her newly acquired knitting machine was her currently most absorbing activity. She began to take a few minutes before starting the machine to become aware of the presence of God, to offer the time and activity as part of her prayer, and to then go on attentively with her knitting. This approach not only expanded her view of what prayer is, but slowly it began to penetrate those other times which were explicitly labelled prayer.

Many Christians are unable to sustain a lengthy prayer time due to the demands of family and work. Often the temptation is to give up altogether, and then feelings of defeat and guilt take over. If there is so little time, why bother? Why not simply admit that, at least during this pressurized period, prayer is not an option? The method used by my schoolteacher friend is available to the busiest person and it brings some surprises. First it helps us to see that there are many different ways in which we can realize the presence of God and lift our hearts in thanksgiving. Then as we pray in association with some enjoyable, absorbing activity, we gain a fresh understanding of God's involvement in all we do. Gradually we learn to find other moments in the day when a brief prayer can be offered, and as we become more conscious of the always present Lord, our attitudes to work, leisure and prayer may begin to change.

I once heard in a sermon the story of a widow with a large family and low income who was renowned for her sanctity. Many came for her practical wisdom, or just to be in the presence of one who so radiated love and hope. Asked when she ever found time to pray, she first looked puzzled, and then replied that she did it all the time; washing dishes, changing diapers, and cooking meals were all expressions of her prayer. The questioner persisted: "But what if you want to be really alone, and just to pray without any of these activities going on?" "Well, then I just throw my apron over my head and I'm alone with the Lord," she answered. This woman had learned what St. Paul meant when he said, "Pray without ceasing."

The seventeenth century monk Brother Lawrence of the Resurrection emphasizes this same attitude to prayer in his book *The Practice of the Presence of God*. The book continues to appeal to readers from widely different traditions because it reflects a spirituality which is accessible to all. Brother Lawrence discovered ways of finding God in the monastery kitchen where he labored among the pots and pans. He did not fill the kitchen with books, but paid attention to what he was doing, offering all his activity as an act of praise to God. Of course, together with the other monks, he had set times of prayer and reading of Scripture, but he did not regard the time of prayer as different from any other, because even the most absorbing work did not divert him from God. He describes his method as "simple attentiveness and a loving gaze on God" and says:

> If I were a preacher, I would preach nothing else but the practice of the presence of God. If I were a director, I would recommend it to everybody: so necessary and even so easy do I believe it to be.[2]

Although his own vocation led him into a monastery where the rhythm of Daily Offices, Eucharist and manual work formed the context of prayer, he recognized that all Christians may practice the presence of God no matter where they were called to be. His advice to those outside the cloister was appropriate for their situation in life. He reassured a woman who could not be in church daily that we are all able to "make a chapel in our heart," and to a soldier seeking his advice he said:

> A little lifting up of the heart is enough, a short remembrance of God, an interior act of worship, made in haste and sword in hand, are prayers which short as they may be, are nevertheless most pleasing to God.[3]

Brother Lawrence did not minimize the problem of distractions, but emphasized that the will, as mistress of our faculties, must be trained to recall the wandering mind, redirecting it to God. If the mind is kept under control at other times, that is, kept in the presence of God, it will be less difficult to be recollected at the time of prayer. And he encourages us to be patient with ourselves. We do not achieve attentiveness all at once, it takes time and practice, and we should not, like a young sister he counselled, try to go faster than grace. Our effort is required, but the other dimension to our growth in prayer is God's gift which cannot be coerced, controlled or hurried. The beauty of Brother Lawrence's spirituality, and that which makes an appeal to us today, is that he sees nothing outside the sphere of God's presence. By paying attention to what is there we honor the Creator, for the most ordinary events and things have the capacity to reveal God to us.

The eighteenth century French Jesuit Jean Pierre de Caussade coined the phrase "the sacrament of the present moment" to speak of the way in which God is hidden yet present in all time, places and activities. The duties which occupy us at each moment he describes as "shadows beneath which the divine action lies concealed."[4] It is by responding to these duties with attention and reverence that the shadows recede, and we catch a glimpse of the reality of God beyond. Prayer involves being present to what is, and abandoning ourselves to the loving providence of God. It is a continuing attitude of trust in God our Creator.

George Herbert expresses the same thought in the poem which has become one of our hymns. God is to be found in all things, and every activity is to be undertaken for God's honor. There is no one, and no thing, too insignificant to praise God. The most humdrum house cleaning task is divinized if it is undertaken for the sake of our Creator:

Teach me my God and King,
In all things thee to see;
And what I do in anything,
To do it as for thee.

All may of thee partake;
Nothing can be so mean,
Which, with this tincture, "for thy sake,"
Will not grow bright and clean.

A servant with this clause
Makes drudgery divine:
Who sweeps a room, as for thy laws,
Makes that and the action fine.

This is the famous stone
That turneth all to gold;
For that which God doth touch and own
Cannot for less be told.[5]

The way we live our lives is both a preparation for, and an extension of, our prayer. If we practice attentiveness in the ordinary things it will be less of a problem when we come to specific times set aside for prayer. God "speaks" in many ways, and learning to listen to the Word in everyday life helps us be attentive to the written Word of God so that we pray it.

There are some other practical ways in which we can prepare ourselves to listen. Creating a space where we pray and making it comfortable and attractive removes some of the grim sense of duty that sometimes accompanies our prayer. Some friends of mine who lived in a rambling old rectory in Scotland took a small box room, painted the walls white, carpeted and furnished it with a small table, candle, bowl of flowers and crucifix. They scattered large, comfortable cushions on the floor. Besides creating a space where the family could gather and offer prayer each morning, it was available to anyone looking for a quiet place in which to pray at other times, a sacred space in which to meditate.

Until recently my own prayer place was a corner of the small studio apartment I occupied in New York City. I had a large comfortable chair in which I sat, and a ceramic oil lamp on the table in front of me which I lit as a prelude to prayer. On the wall was a replica of the cross from St. Damian's Church in Assisi, a constant reminder of the much loved and little emulated Saint Francis whose simplicity, devotion and love for creation are ideals I need constantly before me. I also had a print of an icon of the Annunciation which depicts Mary resisting God's message before she says "yes" to the joy and pain of her vocation as the bearer of Christ. It kept my own ambivalence about God's call before me and reminds me still that I need to go on repeating my "yes" to life.

Before I began to pray each morning I made a large mug of coffee (caffeine helped me to wake up!) and spent about five minutes relaxing, becoming aware of how I felt, of what my body was telling me, and of how I was experiencing God at that moment. I then tried to pray out of that awareness, inviting the Lord to share the feelings and to help me become more attentive to the Word. Then I took time to become centered, quiet and ready to listen. Posture is important, for we pray with our bodies as well as our minds. Releasing tension from the body by concentrating for a few moments on relaxing each part, and establishing a deep, regular breathing pattern, will help in the preparation. One of our problems with prayer stems from the assumption that we can simply switch ourselves on the moment we choose. We spend time and energy getting ready to go out on a date, to go to work or meet friends, but expect to be rewarded with an awareness of God's presence the moment we settle down to prayer. Until we become much more proficient at the practice of the presence of God in all our activities, this process of getting ready will be necessary. It is so simple and basic, yet quite new to many Christians. I recently received a letter from a retired priest who attended a meditation workshop which I had led. He wrote to express his thanks for the breathing and relaxation exercises we had done together as a preparation for meditation. All his life he had carried a burden of guilt, which none of his spiritual directors or confessors had been able to remove, because he was so distracted when he tried to pray. No one had ever suggested that taking time to get ready would help!

Having spent time preparing ourselves for prayer, how do we then listen to the Scriptures and pray them? The old monastic tradition of spiritual reading, which did not mean reading books about prayer, but pondering the *lectio divina*, the divine Word, has much to teach us today. There were three stages in this form of prayer: *lectio* (reading), *meditatio* (meditation), and *oratio* (prayer). The basic activity was lectio, the reading of Scripture, slowly and with deliberation so that the sacred text was really heard. This was done in the liturgy when the community gathered for worship, and far more reflective time was provided in the services than is usual in churches today. The monks also read alone, usually aloud, because the eyes and voice were to be involved in this process. St. Benedict, the father of Western monasticism, specifically instructs those monks who choose to read during siesta to do so in such a way that others are not disturbed! As they spoke the sacred words the body also entered into the action, expressing the text so that it became an integral part of themselves.

The next step was meditatio, during which the text was pondered, tasted, savored, and ruminated upon by repetition, so that it became fixed in memory. It was, in fact,

> an intense reflection upon the text directed principally toward practical application and a memorization of the text to imprint it firmly upon the mind so that it can be recalled later.[6]

This process was indispensable for the opus Dei, the work of God, which included not only the prayer but the manual labor of the monks, during which the meditatio could continue. Oratio followed naturally from the preceding steps and St. Benedict insists that prayer be short and "pure," by which he means free from distractions. Since he knew only too well that it is not possible to remain without distractions for long periods, he encouraged brief, but frequent prayer which would continue throughout the day. When oratio takes place, the purpose of lectio divina has been accomplished:

> There comes a moment when we shut the book, when our eyes close and the soul opens up to God in an intimate dialogue; a dialogue perhaps quite silent, or of few words—non clamosa voce, says St. Benedict,

echoing the Gospel—a dialogue that is rather a simple consent to the words read, savored and loved and
to God who speaks them.[7]

This well-tried method of reading the Scripture has much
to offer us today. We begin by choosing a passage, preferably not
more than eight to ten verses, and reading it slowly aloud. There
really is a lot to be said for hearing the words articulated, since
most of the time we read for information, skimming the text as
we go. The impact and meaning of the passage is greater if our
voices enter into the process. After a pause for reflection the
same verses are read again, still with slow and careful deliberation. During this second reading it often happens that we become more focused on the meaning of the words and more
aware of how they affect us. A third reading will usually lead to
deeper association with some, perhaps one, main thought, and
that can then be the source of meditation. Finally "oratio" can
take place. Out of the rumination on the text some specific
prayer or petition, thanksgiving, penitence or intercession may
be offered. In this way what is heard becomes part of what we
are. This kind of praying can take place during other activities
like commuting to work, or doing chores.

The Psalms are very appropriate for this kind of prayer,
and people can be introduced to the method in a group setting. I
remember meditating on the first few verses of Psalm 139 in this
way at a meditation workshop. The leader read the verses and
then asked me to read them, so that a different voice would be
heard. He offered some guidance for our thoughts. This Psalm
speaks of God searching out and knowing each of us intimately,
knowing our journeying and our resting, being acquainted with
all our ways. The Psalmist realizes that there is no place where
God is not. Even the darkness does not provide a place in which
to hide. The leader invited us to be aware of our feelings as we
thought of God's all-seeing presence. When we shared some of

the experience later, it was interesting to hear of the great comfort some derived from this awareness, and the near terror of others. It became clear that where we were in our experience of and relationship to God influenced our response. Sometimes it is comforting to know that God is near, but often we wish to forget this because we are not sure we want to be confronted by the divine presence. Awareness of our reaction leads to prayer. An expression of gratitude for God's presence, or a request for strength to overcome the fear of intimacy. Maybe we need to ask for guidance to discern where we are on our journey, or consent to remain in the darkness which is also filled with God's presence.

Following the old Benedictine pattern of prayer enables us to enter more fully into the ancient, yet contemporary, Scriptures. We may decide to select a short phrase which has emerged from the reading and carry it with us as we go to the work of the day. "You trace my journeys and my resting places" (Ps. 139:2), remembered in the busyness of employment, might well lead to some fresh attitudes and further short (pure) prayer. In this way the Bible is not simply read but truly prayed, because its truth has been assimilated, and become part of the one who prays. The value of the Bible lies not in our learning about it and pronouncing on it, but in what we become as a result of entering into the sacred text.

In the first creation story of Genesis, God speaks and things come to be. Light, life, the earth, the heavens and humankind are created, and God says, "It is very good." God's word is living, dynamic, and powerful, and it brings beautiful things into existence. When the writer of the Fourth Gospel was searching for a way to speak of the life-transforming presence of Christ, he spoke of him as the divine logos, the Word of God, who brings light and fullness of life to the world. The Prologue of St. John's gospel, strongly reminiscent of the opening chapter of Genesis, introduces us to the incarnate Word who chooses to enter the chaos and darkness of human experience. And there, in the words of Charles Wesley:

> He speaks, and list'ning to his voice,
> New life the dead receive,
> The mournful broken hearts rejoice,
> The humble poor believe.

Jesus gives to those who hear and respond "power" (authority) to become children of God (Jn. 1:12). We learn what it means to share intimacy in the family of God by listening to the Word tell us who we are.

Bible reading can become a unifying principle in our interior life, especially if we adopt the meditative approach to it. An intelligent reading of the Scriptures and serious biblical criticism does not rob us of the sacred text or its capacity to "speak" to us. It is important to understand that the Bible message is for all the people of God, but that we are invited to participate in and apply its truth to our individual lives. As we respond to the text in a spirit of prayerfulness, relaxation and humility, we find ourselves there.

At the end of my prayer time each morning I usually spend a few moments recording thoughts and reflections which have emerged from the Scriptures. Doing so not only establishes them more fully in my consciousness but also opens up further insights. The writing is a process in which I come to understand more fully the implications of what I have read, and it often beckons me in a new direction. It may be that I need to change a particular response to life, or a fresh way of relating to others sometimes opens up, or a new understanding of the reality of God expands my vision and calls for action. Then the Word has again fulfilled the creative purpose; things have changed because the voice of God was heard.

When a phrase or passage of Scripture comes alive for us, it is important to stay with it instead of rushing on because we, or the lectionary, have decided to read more. Bible Study aids or lectionaries are useful in as far as they provide a structure for our reading and prayer, but it is possible to become imprisoned by them. The purpose of reading Scripture is to hear the Lord, and when that happens, we need to stop and listen long enough to respond. A monastic priest friend of mine tells of his experience reading the Office of Vespers one evening when he was away from his community. After the opening sentences the ancient hymn *Phos Hilaron* (O Gracious Light) is sung. The hymn celebrates the biblical concept of Christ as the Light of the World, penetrating the world's darkness, bringing vision and life. That evening he recited the opening words "O gracious Light" and got no further. God, who is pure light, shone in his consciousness in such a way that the only appropriate response was adoration. Momentarily he considered finishing the Office because that was what he had set out to do, but instead consented to stay with what was happening. The Office had achieved its purpose, to reveal the presence of the Lord, and it would have been inappropriate to move on out of a sense of duty.

These moments, when God touches our lives in a special way, are beautiful and encouraging. They support our journey and inspire our prayers. Much of the time, however, we do not find the Scriptures exhilarating and we read without being gripped by what we hear. It is then that the repetition of a short verse or phrase will help us as we try to pray. The use of a mantra is well attested to in the mystical tradition of both East and West, and it enables the pray-er to remain focused and to be faithful in prayer even when the rewards are not apparent. Those in the Judeo-Christian tradition have meditated on Scripture this way, celebrating in their repetition of a phrase some aspect of God's goodness and presence in the world. The following are some suggestions of appropriate mantra sayings for repetition:

Bless the Lord, O my soul
and all that is within me bless his holy name. (Ps. 103:1)

The Lord is my shepherd, I shall not want. (Ps. 23:1)

As a hart longs for flowing streams,
so longs my soul for thee, O God. (Ps. 42:1)

Be still, and know that I am God. (Ps. 46:10)

O give thanks to the Lord, for he is good,
for his steadfast love endures for ever. (Ps. 136:1)

Fear not, for I have redeemed you;
I have called you by name, you are mine. (Is. 43:1)

My soul magnifies the Lord,
and my spirit rejoices in God my Savior. (Lk. 1:46-47)

The Word became flesh and dwelt among us. (Jn. 1:14)

I AM the Bread of Life. (Jn. 6:35)
the true Vine. (Jn. 15:1)
the Way, the Truth and the Life. (Jn. 14:6)
the Resurrection and the Life. (Jn. 11:25)
I AM the Light of the World. (Jn. 8:12)

He is the image of the invisible God,
the firstborn of all creation. (Col. 1:15)

Holy, holy, holy is the Lord God almighty,
who was, and is, and is to come. (Rev. 4:8)

As we repeat the words of Scripture in this way, a rhythm of prayer is established, and this will often penetrate other activities. We may find ourselves walking along the street or waiting for the subway, and the phrase will come back into our minds reminding us that we can pray wherever we happen to be. It also raises our awareness of the Lord at times when our minds were occupied with other things. It is far more productive to be mentally repeating our biblical mantra than rehearsing our irritation that the train is late or the line too long!

Hearing the Word means encounter with the eternal Lord. Sometimes our response must be silence; sometimes we need simply to wait in God's holy presence. Whether we are invited to prostrate ourselves in worship, dance our joy, confess our infidelity, or reaffirm our discipleship we will be changed by what we hear. The transformation which takes place through this dialogue is summarized by Thomas Merton in his little book *He is Risen*, where the existential dimensions of our life in Christ are celebrated so powerfully:

> True encounter with Christ
> liberates something in us,
> a power
> we did not know we had;
> a hope,
> a capacity for life,
> a resilience,
> an ability to bounce back,
> when we thought
> we were completely defeated,
> a capacity to grow
> and change,
> a power
> of creative transformation.[8]

SEEING THE LORD

Mystical experience begins with an invitation.[1]

In previous chapters much of our attention has been focused on the importance of preparation, study and discipline if we are to pray the Bible authentically today. In other words, we recognize that our will is involved in this process, it does not simply happen without some effort on our part. But this is only half the story. Whenever we reach out to the Lord we are responding, whether we know it or not, to a gracious invitation. Prayer begins with desire, with a longing for truth, meaning, and fulfillment and is a response to the divine restlessness that exists in each one of us. It is a response to God's invitation to find our place in the universe and in the divine love.

Mystical experience is not reserved for a few giants in the religious quest, but is a fundamental human experience which has been present throughout history in all cultures. It becomes a reality when we hear and answer God's call. It is

> a living and burning reality that arises in the human
> breast and can only be described in symbolical lan-
> guage. It is what St. John of the Cross powerfully
> calls a living flame of love.[2]

For some of God's people the call and response are dramatic and overwhelming. St. Paul fell to the ground and temporarily lost his sight before he truly "saw" the Lord and found the direction of his life totally reversed. Amos experienced God's voice as the roar of the lion which compelled him to prophesy against a people whose choice of oppression and injustice as a way of life meant they were doomed. To others God speaks more gently. The boy Samuel was awakened by a persistent voice in the night;

Elijah recognized the voice of God not in earthquake, wind or fire but in a still, small voice on the mountain top. Mary, weeping in the garden after the crucifixion of Jesus, saw him for who he was when he gently spoke her name. So God's call comes to us in the variety of our experience, in the extremes of our need, and in the intensity of our emotional life. It also comes to us in the dull, lifeless moments when we feel nothing but our own emptiness. And it comes not once, but many times, spoken as the gift which makes possible our response as we hear and see the Lord.

The prophet Jeremiah heard God's call and responded to it over a period of some forty years. Images from his book can be a rich source for our prayer. Jeremiah exercised his ministry between the years 627 and 587 B.C., a period of turmoil and political unrest in the ancient Near East. Some knowledge of the context in which he spoke will help us to understand his message and its impact. During the tenth century the descendants of those who left Egypt in the Exodus finally became welded into a nation. Following the choice of the charismatic young warrior Saul as leader (a choice that was perceived as a disastrous rejection of Yahweh by some writers and a fulfillment of the divine purpose by others), David was chosen as king over the nation. Under him the kingdom was extended geographically. Jerusalem—a former Jebusite stronghold—established as the capital, and a major building program begun. A royal palace was constructed in Jerusalem, and plans made for building the Temple, which was to become the center of Israel's worship.

When David died in 961 B.C. his son Solomon came to the throne, and he vigorously pursued the major construction work of his father. In addition Solomon established a huge smelting works in Ezion Geber and imported large numbers of chariots and horses from Egypt, which he stabled at Megiddo in the north. In order to provide labor for all this development he introduced conscription, and so fanned into flame the smouldering unrest which had begun in his father's day, especially among the tribes in the north who provided the bulk of the forced labor. The Temple was built and dedicated with great ceremony, but even while the nation rejoiced that Yahweh finally had a home in its midst, civil unrest grew. With the succession of Rehoboam, Solomon's son, it erupted.

Under the leadership of Jeroboam, who had been given charge of the forced labor, the northern tribes came to the new king asking for easier conditions. Rehoboam refused, threatening instead to increase pressure, and a military coup quickly followed. The kingdom was divided, Jeroboam becoming king over the northern territory now called Israel, and Rehoboam retaining the smaller, southern section of Judah.

The history of the next two hundred years is largely one of hostility and intrigue between the two kingdoms and their allies, with occasional interludes of rapprochement. As a means of establishing political and religious independence in the north, shrines were built at Bethel and Dan to replace Temple worship on Mount Zion in Jerusalem. Omri, successor to Jeroboam I, established his capital at Samaria, which also became a heavily fortified city. Internal power struggles continued while pressure from the developing "super-powers" on her borders persisted, and one king followed another in rapid and bloody succession. Syria was a force to be reckoned with until Assyria gained ascendancy, moving ever closer to Israel. When the Syrian capital fell it was only a matter of time before the northern kingdom was besieged.

In 722 B.C. Israel came to an end amidst scenes of terrible violence, destruction, torture and desecration. The biblical writers, recording events largely from a southern perspective, viewed this devastation as the judgment of Yahweh on an evil nation. The loss of the Temple, compromise with foreign worship, and rejection of religious and political unity centered in the Davidic monarchy, were regarded as the cause of divine punishment. When Assyria failed in its attempt to destroy Jerusalem, complacency grew in the nation. Judah had established the line of David, liturgy and kingship were deeply interrelated, and a complex priestly system developed. The kings of Judah often cooperated with the priestly and prophetic leaders of their day, whereas those in the north had been in opposition to the prophets. Isaiah of Jerusalem was a highly respected adviser to King Hezekiah.

The southern kingdom was not without its enemies and political/religious conflicts, but it enjoyed a far greater degree of stability than the north. Geographical location played a significant part in this relative peacefulness. Into this political climate Jeremiah was driven by the urgency of God's call. Isaiah had seen the superficiality of much of Judah's religious ceremonial, and had challenged her complacent trust in the inviolability of the Temple. He tried to recall the nation to a faith based on integrity, justice, and a humble trust in the Creator, whose compassion reaches beyond the bounds of nationalism. Few listened. Jeremiah was to take up the prophet's mantle and to become the voice of Yahweh in the turbulent years which saw an end to the southern kingdom, and the exile of God's people in Babylon. Even then his task was not complete, for it fell to him, far from home, to inject fresh hope and courage in those who were ready to despair.

Jeremiah was not overjoyed at the prospect of a prophetic vocation which would take him from the security of home and the priestly context in which his father ministered. In the opening chapter, Jeremiah offers his youthfulness as an excuse for not responding to God's call. He did not want this task and tried to escape it. The invitation of God creates resistance because it is a call to change and vulnerability and we have a basic urge to avoid both. Our desire for structures and our fear of chaos play a significant part in our reactions to the possibility of moving on and of relating in new ways. When the call comes, however, it is important to let go of our current perceptions and expectations, or we may fall into the sin of idolatry through our unwillingness to relinquish our current image of the Lord. At the same time we are attracted, drawn irresistibly into a "yes" response despite ourselves. So Jeremiah found himself the spokesperson of Yahweh, often at odds with the society of his day, frequently battered, afraid, and disappointed with the Lord. Two passages known as the confessions of Jeremiah (15:17-18, 20:7-18) are a bitter cry of despair in which Jeremiah curses the day of his birth and compares God to a deceitful brook whose waters fail. In his book there is a poignant and profound testimony to the human experience of desire for God and resistance to the divine will. It is the honest story of one who was both prophet and mystic, deeply in touch with divine truth about himself and the nation, and courageously proclaiming it.

A number of powerful images and symbols from the prophecy of Jeremiah can help us in our own praying of the Bible if we open ourselves to the Lord who invites us into intimacy through them. The first of these appears in chapter one immediately after the prophet's call:

> The word of the Lord came to me saying, "Jeremiah, what do you see?" and I said, "I see a rod of almond." Then the Lord said to me, "You have seen well, for I am watching over my word to perform it." (Jer. 1:11-12)

As Jeremiah looks about him he notices a rod of almond blooming, and what he actually sees gives rise to an inner vision. The almond tree was the first to blossom in the spring and was known as the "wake up tree." There is a subtle pun in these verses arising out of the Hebrew root of the words "almond" and "watch," and this becomes a vehicle of God's message. The

Lord too is awake, watching over the word spoken so that it comes to be. Jeremiah's task is a formidable one. He is to issue a call to repentance: Yahweh *will* bring to fulfillment the word spoken. A necessary breaking process will precede healing and Jeremiah's ministry is described in these terms:

> I have set you this day over nations and kingdoms, to pluck up and to break down, to destroy and to overthrow, to build and to plant.(1:10)

Jeremiah might not like his task, but there is a compulsion about it and he is to be the human instrument to make known the divine will.

This first image from the book of Jeremiah can become an important focus for our own meditation. What does it mean to us that God "neither slumbers nor sleeps," but is inextricably involved in our attempts to live out our vocation? This image appears at the beginning of Jeremiah's ministry and represents his own "waking up." What are some of the things which I need to wake up to? Are there injustices in my society? Do complacency, pride, or selfishness exist in me and if so, what am I going to do about it? Are my eyes open so that I too can live prophetically?

Hearing and seeing are closely linked in the prophetic vocation. Those who hear God have a fresh perception of the way things are, and they need to give voice to this insight. Thus prophets are truly mystics, and in each of us who seek to know God the mystic and prophet is birthed. We too see with new eyes and proclaim with fresh conviction.

Most of the images in Jeremiah are drawn from the natural order of things, from his immediate environment. God spoke to him and through him as Jeremiah paid attention to what was there. A boiling stewpot, a hot wind from the desert, a lion from the forest, a grapevine, a misshapen vase in the hands of the potter, a waistcloth buried in the cleft of a rock, an incurable sickness, all "speak" to the prophet of some deeper reality.

All genuine education is a waking up to reality and truth; it involves a growing awareness of what was not necessarily self-evident without paying attention. Education is a drawing forth of what is deep within, a recognition of our own depths, our own wisdom. This is the mystical path, for

> ... mysticism does not mean that we learn new things, but that we learn to know in a new way.[3]

Jeremiah looked at a boiling pot, probably someone's evening meal bubbling over in a northerly direction (1:13-14). As he looked the pot became a further sign of God's judgment, and of the Assyrian threat on Judah's northern borders. Again he saw in a simple, ordinary occurrence, God's message to the nation.

Sometimes Jeremiah was called upon to incorporate acted parables in his proclamation of judgment. In chapter 19 God told him to buy a potter's earthen flask and then to go with some of the elders and senior priests to the Potsherd Gate in the Valley of Hinnom. There he was to smash the pot as a sign of the destruction to come. This dramatic sermon created much hostility, and, consequently the priest Pashhur had Jeremiah beaten and placed in the stocks as a punishment. The cost of the call was high! This account is preceded by the story of Jeremiah going to a potter's house and watching the craftsman at work:

> I went down to the potter's house, and there he was working at his wheel. And the vessel he was making of clay was spoiled in the potter's hand, and he reworked it into another vessel, as it seemed good to the potter to do. Then the word of the Lord came to me: "O house of Israel, can I not do with you as this potter has done? says the Lord." (18:3-5)

The sermon which marked him out as a disturber of the peace may well have grown out of this earlier observation. The wet clay, pliable in the potter's hand, could be reworked; God had not yet abandoned the people and hope was not entirely lost. Jeremiah no doubt needed this reassurance as he executed his unenviable task of alerting the nation to God's judgment. Often the initial insight which emerges in our meditation, will grow into further ideas, some of which demand action we would prefer to avoid. Then our praying of the Scriptures takes place as we *do* what we believe God is asking of us. This is not a time for reflection and waiting, but the decisive moment in which to act. Prophets, because they "see" God's truth, become illuminators; the light of God is manifested through them to others. God is constantly reminding us to wake up, to take responsibility, and to make choices which not only affect our lives, but the society in which we live. Our initial reaction may be similar to Jeremiah's, "I can't," and we may offer any number of plausible-sounding excuses to avoid the prophetic imperative of the mystical experience. But the awakening is also a call to conversion and change. It involves a discovery of our mission, and a movement from "I can't" to "I will." Self-knowledge and awareness begin to happen when we let go of apathy and wake up—when we begin to see with God's eyes, and, energized by God's powerful Word/Spirit, speak God's truth.

The interior call and the waking up process plunged Jeremiah into action and commitment to truth and justice. Vision means involvement; it means confronting all that prevents or perverts justice in God's world. It is a costly call, since it challenges the status quo and therefore invites hostility, and Jeremiah had more than his share of opposition. Placed in the stocks to be ridiculed, cast into a disused water cistern to die of starvation in the mire, attacked, resented, he remained faithful—and sane. He did not pretend to enjoy all this; at times he raged at God, struggled with his desire to escape and gave way to his paranoia, but in the honest expression of doubt, anger, resentment and fear lay the key to psychological and spiritual health.

The rest of the book of Jeremiah is very rich in images and experiences which touch our own lives. We can pray the Bible by allowing the images of those who struggled to respond to God in their day speak to us. More than this, we can begin to practice the art of attention, of waking up to the things around us so that they become the focus of new seeing and hearing.

We make a mistake, however, if we think that God speaks only in the tranquility of the natural order, or if we see only tranquility there. The chain of birth, growth, struggle, survival and death is also part of creation and we close our eyes to reality if we ignore it. Never was this more jarringly made clear to me than during a time of retreat at a contemplative monastery deep in the pine woods of South Carolina. The hum of insects and birdsong were suddenly shattered as jets flown for practice to carry nuclear warheads screamed across the sky just above the trees. Then the baying of hounds interrupted the morning quiet, for this was the hunting season. This incursion of the myth that the countryside is where peace reigns was healthy, for unless we allow the painful realities of our broken world to invade and become part of our prayers, we place a limit on where we are willing to allow God to address us. God speaks in the, city too, in the ghetto, the subway, the unemployment office, and on the streets which many are compelled to call home. As we contemplate the images around us every day, God makes visible the intricate web of relationships in which we are all involved, and it is in this context that we must do our living and praying.

Keeping our eyes open for street signs, buildings, garbage containers, and store fronts, as well as the people who inhabit our cities, may produce some surprising images through which the Lord will address us. Traveling on the upper deck of a red London bus one day, I was suddenly struck by a sign high up on a building. "CLUTCH CLINIC" it said, indicating that the gas station below specialized in repairing and replacing defective auto clutches. However, that was not what the sign said to me; it became instead the word of the Lord, as I reflected on the things in my life which I hold on to with such determination. It was an invitation from God to do some letting go, to relinquish the self-image I wanted to preserve, to release some attitudes I had held on to for many years, and to allow some changes in my life style. That sign became the focus for my prayers and my journal for several weeks as slowly I opened the tightly closed fists which wanted to hold on to what was now obsolete. The sign led to a further image, that of the three-year-old child whose fingers are curled tightly around the candy she does not want to share, but who is unable to enjoy it as long as it remains squeezed into a hidden, sticky mess.

There is great beauty to be found in the city, too. The weed which pushes its way through the concrete sidewalk speaks of the power of life to break through the hardness of oppression. The dozen or so pigeons, perched on the arm of a street light high above the grid-locked traffic, seem to tell us to laugh at ourselves a little, we who are so serious, so rushed, beating ourselves into frantic impatience—for what? When they have had enough of it all the pigeons take off, free, moving on wind currents until they find some new vantage point from which to mock our frenetic activity. The wonderful New York Deli owner, who always has the capacity to make his customers believe that life is worth living is often an inspiration to me, calling forth prayers of thanksgiving. An immigrant from a totalitarian state, he overflows with gratitude that he is now a citizen of the United States who, through constant hard work and long hours in his shop, is able to provide modestly for his family. He treats every customer with respect and kindness, and is particularly generous to the many street people who patronize his store. To meet him means to feel valued, to be given the gift of hope out of which to celebrate life.

Wherever God has called us to be at this moment is the place for us to become mystics and prophets. We do this by simply paying attention and asking ourselves, "What does this mean to me? What do I see and what must I say, by my life as well as my lips, as a result of this seeing?" Meditating on the biblical prophets and on the images they offer is an excellent way to be in touch with our own capacity to make connections between things. We pray the Bible as we use their insights, and our praying expands to include our own image-making, too.

LIVING THE QUESTIONS

Live the questions now.

Towards the end of 1902 Francis Xavier Kappus, a student of the Military Academy in Wiener-Neustadt, discovered the poetry of Rainer Maria Rilke, who had preceded him at that institution by some eight years. Kappus had begun to compose verse in response to an inner creative urge, and now wrote to Rilke in order to to share his personal story and to ask for an opinion on his poetry. The correspondence which followed—ten letters written over five years—reveal the spiritual wisdom and stature of the older man. The young poet discovered in him more than a literary critic; Rilke became the spiritual guide who enabled him to grow through the turbulence of searching and doubt. In the fourth letter, written from Worpswede on July 16th 1903, Rilke offers this counsel to Kappus:

> You are so young, so before all beginning, and I want
> to beg you, as much as I can, dear sir, to be patient
> toward all that is unsolved in your heart and to try to
> love the questions themselves like locked rooms and
> like books that are written in a very foreign tongue.
> Do not now seek the answers, which cannot be given
> you because you would not be able to live them. Live
> the questions now. Perhaps you will then gradually,
> without noticing it, live along some distant day into
> the answer.[1]

Learning to be patient toward all that is unsolved in the human heart means accepting that we are unfinished. We are not whole, complete people but people who are in the process of becoming. We are provisional people, affected by the many vicissitudes of life. Most of us do not find the patience enjoined by Rilke readily accessible, and the spectre of fear looms as we experience the tensions of our incompleteness. The temptation then is to bury the fear and refuse the questions. If we opt for avoidance, however, we deny a central element of human nature—our unsolved fragmentation.

The gospels represent Jesus as the asker of questions. He refuses to provide easy answers, which take away the human responsibility to search for truth. The response he makes to those who want rules compels them to "live the questions" in the light of the one command which is central to his teaching: "Love God with all your being and your neighbor as yourself."[2] One of the ways in which we can pray the Bible in our own day is by listening to the questions Jesus asks and by living our way into a response. Each of the gospels provides examples of Jesus' questions which are significant for us, but the Fourth Gospel is especially rich in examples of fundamental questions. The author sees Jesus as the Revealer of God, the one who leads his hearers deeper inside themselves as they search for meaning. The revelation takes place when people struggle with doubt, when they face their own reality, when they allow themselves to be placed in question.

Jesus' first words in St. John's gospel are in the form of a question: "What do you seek?" (1:38). He is addressing the disciples of John, who now turn from their master and follow him to whom the Baptist bore witness. The evangelist makes it clear that John must withdraw into the wings, for, as he says in 3.30, "He must increase but I must decrease." The Revealer of God, who also reveals people to themselves, comes under the floodlights and those who follow him are invited to identify the object of their search, to clarify the purpose of their journey.

Few external details are given about the meeting between the disciples of John and Jesus. To the writer of this gospel the details are not of primary importance, for he uses people and incidents to present timeless realities and as a way of inviting the reader to encounter the eternal Christ. The author writes to evoke faith in those who hear or read the gospel. The question is all important: "What do you seek?" The scholar A.E. Harvey has suggested that the Gospel of John has been constructed as a trial. The witnesses are assembled—individuals as well as the words and works of Jesus—and all testify to his glory. But the verdict is left open, for we, the readers, are judge and jury.[3] Ultimately, however, we judge ourselves by our response to the truth manifested in Jesus.

The first question which Jesus asks places us at the beginning of our search. "What do you seek?" It is the starting-point for all who seek the truth and, Bultmann suggests,

> It is clearly the first question which must be addressed by anyone who comes to Jesus, the first thing about which he must be clear. And it is essential to know where Jesus lives; for in the place where Jesus is at home the disciple will also receive his dwelling.[4]

The two disciples of John had learned well from their master, who pointed them away from himself and toward Jesus. They began to follow Jesus but their understanding and purpose were not yet defined. What did they seek? Perhaps it was their very lack of clarity which led them to ask their own question: "Rabbi, where are you staying?" The disciples could not yet define the object of their search, but at least they could discover where they might continue to find Jesus. His "Come and see" was met with immediate response and they remained in his company for the rest of the day.

Nothing is disclosed about the content of their conversation with Jesus, or of their future as his disciples. It is enough for us to know that the answer to the question "What do you seek?" is a person, not an object. Remaining with Jesus, spending time where he lives, is essential for the journey of faith. And the question is as relevant to the present-day disciple as it was to those who first heard it. As we place ourselves in the presence of the living Word of God, we are invited to tell him why we are there. What is it that we are looking for? What do we want from him? How do we experience ourselves when we are confronted by searching questions which demand honesty? In the process of exploring the first question new ones open up, and we see that our responses will need to be repeated as fresh insights are gained, for remaining where Jesus is constitutes not only the beginning of the journey, but also its continuation. Jesus is the Way, as the author tells us in 14:6, and with him fresh vistas of life, faith and self-understanding open up as we travel.

Another important question occurs in the third chapter of the gospel, when John records the nocturnal visit to Jesus of the Pharisee, Nicodemus. Narrative is reduced to a minimum in this section and Nicodemus never even states his purpose in coming, but the author uses the incident to express the radical nature of believing in Jesus. Learned argument will not suffice; baptism by water alone is inadequate; only a new birth, *anothen*, from above, enables a person to enter the Kingdom of God. Nicodemus is incredulous. Even with his professional knowledge of the Scriptures, he is not able to grasp that Jesus is speaking of the fulfillment of Old Testament hopes. So Jesus asks: "Are you a teacher in Israel, and yet you do not understand this?" (3:10) A radically new interpretation of the tradition and of life is called for.

By suggesting in his opening statement that Nicodemus is excluded from the sphere of God unless he becomes a new person, Jesus invites Nicodemus to call his own life into question. Who am I? Where do I belong? Clearly in the human sphere anything like a rebirth is impossible, and something more than improvement is required. This is not an action which Nicodemus can perform for himself; he needs a new origin, and this is pure gift. In the discourse that follows, the reader hears the Johannine community speaking—"We speak of what we know"—and the context appears to be the contemporary dialogue between church and synagogue. However we too are addressed in our time and place: "Do you understand this? Have you grasped the radical nature of believing, understood that it involves a change of origin, entry into a new sphere?" The thought of these verses was present in the Prologue: "To all who received him, who believed in his name, he gave power to become children of God; who were born, not of blood...nor of the will of man, but of God" (1:12-13). We are invited to place ourselves in question, to believe in Jesus, to be born of the spirit and thus to experience God's gift of eternal life.

The operation of the *Pneuma* (Spirit) is bound by no discernible law and only its effect provides evidence of its presence. None can deny the reality of the wind, although it is incomprehensible, and no one knows where it comes from or where it goes. So it is with the Spirit. The Spirit of God moves inscrutably in the Church and in the lives of individuals. These verses warn against constructing rigid formulas for defining those who are "born again;" they challenge us to be flexible and responsive to the continuing initiatives of God's Spirit in our lives.

We experience ambiguity in our dealings with God and with others, and often we fearfully try to resist it. This is not an appropriate response to our spiritual quest, for we are dealing with God who is Mystery. We cannot define, contain, and comprehend God or the movement of God's Spirit. The ambiguity is there to be embraced; to become part of what we are. We are dramatically changed as we remain with Christ, and some of the change takes place as we tentatively approach him in the darkness and find him increasing our sense of incomprehension. We pray the Bible as we are addressed by similar questions to those asked Nicodemus. "Are you a Christian of long standing? A

Sunday school teacher? A minister of the Gospel? And still you don't understand these things? How far have you allowed radical change to take place in your life? How open are you to the new movements of the Spirit disturbing the familiar categories by which you shape your life?"

In the Gospel of John a careful selection of the "mighty works" of Jesus is made, and these are called signs because they point away from themselves to the Revealer. Their purpose is to evoke faith. The third of these signs is recorded in chapter five, and it contains a question which is far more searching than might be evident at first glance. The story focuses on the healing of a man whose sickness had incapacitated him for thirty years. The scene is a pool near the sheepgate in Jerusalem, locally called Bethzatha. Here invalids waited in the five porticos for the water to be "troubled." A gloss on the text tells us that an angel of the Lord was responsible for this, and that whoever stepped first into the water following the movement was cured. Jesus saw the unnamed sick man and asked: "Do you want to be healed?"

The Revealer does not compel people to take his way, but draws their gaze away from the hopelessness of their own solutions. This sick man turned his eyes from the pool to Jesus and hearing the imperious summons, "Take up your pallet and walk," experienced immediate healing. Unable to give a satisfactory reply to those critics who objected to healing on the Sabbath, the healed man went to the temple. Here Jesus found him and reassured him about his cure, adding "Sin no more," thus linking his healing with forgiveness. Again, John tells us nothing about the future of this man; he has served his purpose in the gospel by revealing human responsibility to consent to Jesus' healing power.

When people encountered Christ they found a new desire to be whole and a new purpose in life. The man at the pool was apparently energized by his meeting with Jesus to do the impossible. He stood up and walked. Blind Bartimaeus, asked by Jesus, "What do you want me to do for you?" responded with the simple yet hope-filled request that his sight might be restored. Each of them was first asked to define what he was really looking for. Through questioning Jesus asks us to distinguish between fantasy and reality in our quest for spiritual growth and wholeness. Sometimes we mask our real desires with high-sounding religious statements about our wants. I recall reading this passage of Scripture at a time when I was feeling particularly hurt and angry because someone had betrayed my trust. There was much bitterness and resentment for which I needed God's healing and forgiveness, but I realized that at that moment I did not want to be healed. I wanted the nasty feeling to go away, and I wanted to see myself responding in a truly Christlike way to the person who had let me down, but I was not yet ready to let go of the hurt which made it impossible for me to really forgive. All I could do was to offer to God the full range of powerful emotion, instead of pretending to possess love and forgiveness, and consent to wait and go on praying until the healing could take place. The answer to the question "Do you want to be healed?" was, for me, "No—what I want is to avoid encountering the dark, unreconciled parts of myself, but I consent to that process and I am willing to wait until I can say "yes" to the question."

Another of Jesus' signs, the healing of a congenitally blind man, is recorded in chapter nine. This also contains a question which is pertinent to us. The whole story is told in a dramatic form which highlights a wide variety of responses to the presence of Jesus. A number of groups appear before we arrive at the question in v. 35: "Do you believe in the Son of Man?" The disciples are represented as a group concerned to arrive at some clear understanding about the cause of the man's affliction; was it his personal sin or that of his parents which caused the blindness? Compassion seems not to enter their thinking, for they are

obsessed with theological questions to which they require answers. The man himself apparently acted immediately to comply
with Jesus' instructions and so was healed. He was unconcerned
with theological issues, though soon to be plunged into contro-
versy about them. For him the important issue was healing, and
he was freed from a lifelong condition which had limited his relationships and activity in the world.

Neighbors were astonished by what had happened; in fact,
they questioned whether this could be the same beggar they had
known for years. Their interest was aroused and they wanted to
meet the one responsible for such a change. Curiosity stimulated
their search, though how seriously they pursued it is not evident.
The guardians of religious orthodoxy soon heard what had happened. Their first concern was with the broken law. Since Jesus
had healed on the Sabbath he must be a sinner, yet there were
some among them reasoned that such a healing could only have
taken place through the power of God. There was division
among them. The parents of the man were called in to establish
his identity and they confirmed that this was indeed their son,
but refused to be drawn into any comment about his healing.
John tells us that they feared excommunication, thus reflecting a
serious threat to the church in his own day. The parents placed
all responsibility on their son, who was again interrogated and
threatened. He replied with wit, biting sarcasm and plain common sense. Dismissing the criticisms leveled at Jesus he simply
bore testimony to his experience: "One thing I know, that
though I was blind, now I see" (9:25).

The decisive question was now put to the formerly blind
man. Jesus finds him and asks: "Do you believe in the Son of
Man?" Jesus' question is designed to contrast two kinds of
recognition. The first has already taken place; Jesus is seen as a
prophet (v. 7), and that is as far as the man can come in the
sphere of natural human reason. If he is to see Jesus for who he

really is, he must move on and take a decisive step of faith. The question is put to him explicitly for by it he is confronted by the self-revelation of the Word. He does not see a further miracle or respond to a command to believe, yet his own experience which was previously obscure, becomes intelligible to him. He can say "Lord I believe" and worship the Revealer. In that instant he moves into the sphere of light.

The struggle between light and darkness, and the cost implied in the decision of faith, are made clear in this chapter. The concluding dialogue between Jesus and the Pharisees ends with the most devastating words in the New Testament, for they are complete reversal of the words of absolution. To those who refuse to see, Jesus says, "Your guilt remains" for they are culpably blind. The Revealer is before them; he confronts them with their own reality and they choose to remain in the sphere of darkness.

The Gospel of John places tragedy and triumph side by side, and the theme is poignantly introduced in the Prologue. Like the figure of Wisdom in the intertestamental literature, especially as depicted in Proverbs 8, the Word offers the light of truth and life in the market place of people's lives. Many refuse it; some respond. But the light is not extinguished and those who receive the Word and believe receive power to become children of God. Whether v. 5 of the Prologue represents the tragic or triumphant response to the light is unclear, and hangs on the interpretation of *katelaben*, the Greek word which can mean either "apprehend," "take hold of," or "to overcome." In the subsequent encounters between the Revealer and those he meets, both responses are found. Chapter nine confronts us with a blind man who sees the light and makes the response of faith, and the Pharisees who refuse the revelation. As Raymond Brown puts it:

> While the former blind man is gradually having his
> eyes opened to the truth about Jesus, the Pharisees

82

> or the Jews are becoming more obdurate in their
> failure to see the truth... The care with which the
> evangelist has drawn his portraits of increasing in-
> sight and hardening blindness is masterful. Three
> times the former blind man, who is truly gaining
> knowledge, confesses his ignorance (12, 25, 36).
> Three times the Pharisees, who are really plunging
> deeper into abysmal ignorance of Jesus, make confi-
> dent statements about what they know of him.[5]

The journey of faith leads us deeper into an understanding
of who Jesus is. Questions about what we believe concerning
Jesus are not adequately answered by reference to credal statements or quotations from the church fathers. The authentic answers must come from deep within ourselves as we reflect on our
own experience of his healing power in our lives. There is a sense
in which we are all to be Gospel writers, telling the good news as
it is for us, celebrating the living Christ who expands our vision
through our daily encounters with him.

The central section of the Gospel of John, especially the
Farewell Discourses in chapters 13-17, contain many questions
and they indicate that there are often times when the disciples
will not have clear answers. Jesus says to his followers: "I have
yet many things to say to you, but you cannot bear them now"
(16:12). They are to wait until the Spirit of truth enlightens them
so that they can make sense of Jesus' words in the light of their
own experience. An important paradigm for our growth in Christ
is contained in a verse which immediately precedes these discourses. It emphasizes the value of waiting in the darkness.
"Truly, truly I say to you, unless a grain of wheat falls into the
earth and dies, it remains alone; but if it dies, it bears much
fruit" (12:24). The context is the willingness to lose one's life in
order to live, and it may well be John's version of the invitation
Jesus makes in the Synoptic Gospels to deny self, to take up the
cross and follow him. John's image, however, emphasizes a di-

mension which is not clearly present in the other versions— that of gestation. A grain of wheat does not "die" and then immediately spring to life but must remain in the darkness of the earth until the time for fruitbearing arrives. Any premature emergence will be disastrous and it will fail to produce the harvest for which it was created. As we consent to remain in the darkness of uncertainty, as we go on praying when we don't have answers, we grow to maturity in Christ. The poet Rilke says:

> Everything is gestation and then bringing forth. To let each impression, and each germ of a feeling come to completion wholly in itself, in the dark, in the inexpressible, the unconscious, beyond the reach of one's own intelligence, and await with deep humility and patience the birth hour of a new clarity; that alone is living the artist's life.[6]

No society has had greater access to the easy, the instant and the quick than our own. We demand immediate gratification, goods or information. And if we indulge our desire to understand, clarify, dogmatize, explain and, by premature solutions to foreclose on the questions which bother us, we will never discover our own mystery; still less will we enter into the mystery of God. Incomprehension is lonely and most of us shrink from being alone. As children we approach the world wisely, without understanding. but then we learn to cover the nakedness of our not-knowing by constructing fig-leaf explanations. Jesus' questions gently but relentlessly challenge our unreality as we pray our way into them.

Following the footwashing in 13:12, Jesus asks a question: "Do you know what I have done for you?" Clearly he is not simply referring to the act of service just performed, but to the meaning of this event, and he has already indicated that full understanding is not yet possible (13:7). It will only become clear in the context of the on-going life of the community that is being brought into being. So Jesus tells the disciples he has acted out for them by example the kind of existing for one another to which they are called. Discipleship is not to be undertaken in isolation from the rest of the community of faith, for privatized religion is a travesty. The question invites the disciples to understand what Dietrich Bonhoeffer later stressed in his ministry to the confessing church in Germany, when it too was experiencing opposition and the darkness of uncertainty:

> Christianity means community through Jesus Christ and in Jesus Christ. No Christian community is more or less than this. Whether it be a brief, single encounter or the daily fellowship of years, Christian community is only this. We belong to one another only through Jesus Christ. What does this mean? It means, first, that a Christian comes to others because of Jesus Christ. It means, second, that a Christian comes to others only through Jesus Christ. It means, third, that in Jesus Christ we have been chosen from eternity, accepted in time, and united for eternity.[7]

The nature of the disciples' fellowship with Jesus is about to change. His death will mean physical absence from them, and the Farewell Discourses are a preparation for his departure. Jesus promises that the Spirit will come to dwell with them to continue his work and to give them power to witness as the community of believers. They are to depend utterly on his word of promise even when they are facing fear, uncertainty and loneliness. He tells them: "It is to your advantage that I go away" (16:7), for he knows that they will only come to realize the fruitfulness of their loneliness if initially it fills them with dismay. Jesus' abandonment of them is temporary and their grief will not last for ever. His absence has purpose. As they live through it, holding on to his words although they feel bereft and alone, they will learn to live in a new dimension of faith.

Clearly many questions continued to occupy the minds of the disciples, sometimes finding expression in their conversation together. In 16:19 we read: "Jesus knew that they wanted to ask him; so he said to them, 'Is this what you are asking yourselves, what I meant by saying, A little while,and you will not see me, and again a little while, and you will see me?' " This leads to a repetition of reassurance, the promise of joy, and the invitation to ask the Father for what they need, for their requests will be granted if made in the name of Jesus.

His followers feel greater confidence at this, but Jesus then says: "Do you now believe? The hour is coming, indeed it has come, when you will all be scattered, every man to his home, and will leave me alone" (16:31-32). Their seeing and understanding are as yet incomplete. It is inappropriate to grasp at the insight they have acquired, for there is much more yet to be revealed to them. He *is* going away. They *do* have to live through the darkness. They must not try to avoid its impact by settling for the provisional understanding they possess now, but allow it to inspire hope in the future that is yet to be made manifest.

Experiences of incomprehension and the absence of any sense experience of the presence of God are difficult to live through. Our natural inclination is to grasp for some new emotional experience to replace the sense of loss. But remaining in the darkness is vital to growth. If we identify ourselves with the disciples of Jesus in their loss, we too can begin to pray the Bible by expressing our fear, anger, and incomprehension to the God who seems absent. This will also enable us to reverse the assumption that God is found in the harmonious, peaceful, unifying parts of our experience, but is absent from the turmoil, terror and fragmentation. We will become more integrated as we pursue our faith journey in the conviction that there is no place where God is not. Doubt will play a significant role in our lives unless we opt for a fantasy religion in which the human struggle for meaning is jettisoned in favor of magic.

The story of Thomas' post-resurrection encounter with Jesus underscores the value of doubt in the life of faith. Thomas was absent from the group of disciples when Jesus first appeared to them. We can only speculate on the reason for this. Maybe he had some pressing business to deal with; perhaps he was disillusioned; possibly he recognized his need for time to reflect, re-evaluate and allow the grieving process to take place. Whatever the reason for his absence, it is clear that the others had a community experience he did not share and at some unspecified point they told Thomas about it. "We have seen the Lord," they said, using the title of the community of faith. He refused to accept their witness without tangible proof—he wanted to see and touch the wounds of Jesus. Did he suspect a hoax, or fear that some kind of hallucination had deluded them? No doubt his refusal to believe their words generated anger, since it could be construed as an attack on their integrity. They would probably feel deep resentment that one who was not present when the first encounter took place now assumed a superior, unbelieving stance. Almost certainly the disciples would feel frustration over their failure to communicate a deeply important, life-transforming experience. The prophetic compulsion to communicate the message of the Lord is characteristic of those who experienced the risen Christ. But Thomas says: "I will not believe."

The following Sunday they were all together, and the atmosphere was charged with emotion. There was expectation—will he come again?—and fear that he might not. The event is described with the same formula as in 20:19: "Jesus came and stood among them and said 'Peace be with you.'" Relief, joy and hope filled Thomas and there was no need for him to respond to the invitation to touch Jesus. The only possible response was a confession of faith, "My Lord and my God," thus turning around his earlier statement, "I will not believe."

The evangelist uses the Thomas incident to exalt a faith not dependent on sight (20:29): "Have you believed because you have seen me? Blessed are those who have not seen and yet believe." At the same time it is evident that those who are honest about the reality of their faith level, and admit to needing supports instead of fantasizing a degree of trust they do not possess, are met by the risen Lord. Christ met Thomas where he was, not where he would like to have been. That encounter was so significant for the disciple that it led to the Gospel's culminating confession of faith. The story encourages us to come to the Lord with our "little faith," thus opening ourselves to the transforming presence of the risen Christ who meets us where we truly are.

In the Epilogue of this gospel we learn that penitence is an essential element in the journey of faith and that we can find recovery and growth through failure. The question that Jesus addresses to Peter reveals the way in which God lovingly probes the wounds of shame before pouring on the oil of healing and forgiveness and hope. This post-resurrection appearance takes place in Galilee. A number of the disciples return to fishing and, after an unsuccessful night, a stranger who stands on the beach tells them to try casting their nets on the other side of the boat. When they do so they make a large catch, and the "beloved disciple" recognizes the stranger as Jesus. Peter hears him say, "It is the Lord," and immediately he springs into the sea to get to Jesus. A charcoal fire is burning and fish and bread await the disciples, who are invited to add some of their catch to the meal.

Following breakfast Jesus addresses Peter: "Simon, son of John, do you love me more than these?" (21:15) The disciple replies: "Yes, Lord, you know that I love you." He is told: "Feed my lambs." The question is twice repeated and on the third occasion we learn that Peter was grieved, although the reason for this is not offered. It is possible that the explanation lies in the choice of the verbs used. Peter is twice asked whether he loves (*agapao*) Jesus and twice replies affirmatively, but substitutes the word *phileo*. In the third question Jesus uses Peter's words, which might suggest that he was even casting doubt upon Peter's kind of loving. It now seems evident that the two verbs for love could be used interchangeably in first century Greek, and interpretation based on a rigid separation of meaning is not conclusive. However we are left with the question of why John chose to distinguish between them. He could simply have been aiming for literary variation, but it is more than possible that he attached a different meaning to them. It certainly offers a plausible alternative to the usual suggestion that Peter was grieved because Jesus repeated the question three times.

Surely it is no accident that the threefold denial of Jesus near a charcoal fire in the courtyard of the High Priest is reversed by a threefold affirmation of love by another charcoal fire. Here Peter learns that failure, though humiliating, is not final, and vocation is not lost. He wept tears of penitence when he made his breach of faith; now forgiveness and restoration can take place. He has learned something more about himself, learned not to overstate his devotion to Jesus, but he is still Simon. He has not yet become Cephas, as predicted by Jesus in 1:42, and quickly moves from Jesus' prophetic utterance about his future to ask about the beloved disciple. What is going to happen to him? Will he die in old age, too? Peter is deflected from his own course by a prying concern about another and is told, in effect, to mind his own business: "If it is my will that he remain until I come, what is that to you? Follow me!" (21:22) Thus the invitation which, according to the Synoptic Gospels, Jesus gave to Peter when they first met, is repeated. Follow me.

Failure need never be final with God. There is always a way forward from where the disciple is at any given moment. In the

Farewell discourses Jesus turned the gaze of the disciples away from the past, which was no more, inviting them to look to the future with its obligations. At the end of the gospel Peter, in many ways the representative of the community of faith, is directed away from the despair of infidelity and pointed toward a hope-filled future into which he will pastor Christ's flock. He is given a commission and given himself.

The need to love and accept ourselves as we are, and the need to forgive ourselves where we are, knowing that God reaches out in love, acceptance and forgiveness, is crucial. For many the sacrament of reconciliation plays an important part in the continuing process of recognizing and owning sin and celebrating God's healing of our brokenness. Peter heard again Christ's affirmation of his vocation when he confronted his own reality. He still had many questions and would make many more mistakes even after he assumed pastoral leadership of the community, but the word of acceptance and hope enabled him to go on. The words "Go in peace, God has put away your sin," invite us to embrace the future with joy.

Living the questions as Jesus lived them, refusing to suppress the doubts, uncertainties and paradoxes of faith, is the way we realize our full humanity. This is how we affirm life as a quest and pray the Scriptures authentically. Henri J. Nouwen's advice to teachers of religion has a much wider application, for it speaks to all who are serious about the life of prayer:

> To disclose the questioning Lord, therefore, requires the humble confession of our basic human ignorance and powerlessness. This is a much needed confession. It is a hard confession because we are living in a world in which success is our ideal as well as our idol; a needed confession because if success becomes the main motivation in life, jealousy, hatred, aggression, violence, and war are the logical consequences . . . .
> When the Lord enters into the center of our lives to

unmask our illusion of possessing a final solution and
to disarm us with always-deeper questions, students
and teachers will not necessarily have an easier or
simpler life, but certainly a life which is honest, and
marked with the on-going search for truth.[8]

The Scriptures live for us because the God to whom they
testify gives them life. The eternal One speaks and invites our response in and through the Word. We come with our academic
credentials or with none, with our doubt or with our faith, our
joy or our fear, and we find that the Bible addresses us where we
are. We hear, digest, and receive its truth deep within ourselves
and then allow it to be poured out in our prayer. The Spirit of
the living God transforms our inarticulate speech and gives us a
heart and mind to praise the Creator. In this reality we live and
grow.

REFERENCES

Bearing the Wound

1. R.S. Thomas *Frequencies* (London: Macmillan, 1978).

Praying the Psalms

All quotations from the Psalms are taken from the Book of Common Prayer of the Episcopal Church.

Knowing the Scriptures

1. The Gospel writers, who in their own day were under pressure from the religious hierarchy—especially the Pharisees—present a very negative image of this group. It is important to remember that the experience of persecution has distorted the truth by focusing on the hypocrisy and hostility of Pharisees to Jesus and the church. In fact, there were among them many sincere and compassionate men, whose leadership was invaluable to the Jewish people during this period of turmoil and intolerance. Certainly their moral principles gave stability and a sense of unity to the nation.

2. Matthew makes even more explicit the identification of Jesus with the figure of Wisdom in his parallel verse in 11:19. He tells us that Wisdom is justified by her deeds, implying that it is the mighty works of Jesus that declare he *is* Wisdom.

Hearing the Word

1. Brother Lawrence, *The Practice of the Presence of God* (Springfield, IL: Templegate, 1974), p. 44.

2. *Ibid.*, p. 61.

3. *Ibid.*, p. 82.

4. J. P. de Caussade, *Self-Abandonment to Divine Providence* (Springfield, IL: Templegate, 1959).

5. George Herbert, "The Elixir," *The Works of George Herbert* (Oxford: Clarendon Press, 1941).

6. Claude Pfeifer, OSB, *Monastic Spirituality* (New York: Sheed and Ward, 1966), p. 396.

7. Jean Leclercq, "Meditation as Biblical Reading," *Worship* 33: 9, p. 565.

8. Thomas Merton, *He is Risen* (New York: Argus Communications, 1975).

Seeing the Lord

1. William Johnston, *The Inner Eye of Love* (San Francisco: Harper and Row, 1978), p. 89.

2. *Ibid.*, p. 90.

3. *Ibid.*, p. 33.

Living the Questions

1. Rainer Maria Rilke, *Letters to a Young Poet* (New York: Norton, 1962), p. 35.

2. Victor P. Furnish, *The Love Command in the New Testament*, (London: SCM, 1973). Furnish examines the centrality of Jesus' command to love, which is attested to by Christian and non-Christian writers of the first two centuries. He traces its presence through all the New Testament writers (not merely the gospels, where the commendation to love is formulated as a command) and shows that by it a community of love is called into being and summoned to responsible action. The complexity of ethical responsibilities to which the community is summoned can only be addressed as each new generation allows its decision-making to be conditioned by the primacy of love commanded by Jesus.

3. A.E. Harvey, *Jesus on Trial: A Study in the Fourth Gospel* (London: SCM, 1976).

4. Rudolf Bultmann, *The Gospel of John* (Oxford: Blackwell, 1971), p. 100.

5. Raymond Brown, *The Gospel according to John* (Garden City, NY: Doubleday, 1966), p. 377.

6. Rilke pp. 29-30.

7. Dietrich Bonhoeffer, *Life Together* (New York: Harper's, 1954), p. 21.

8. Henri Nouwen, "Living the Questions: The Spirituality of the Religion Teacher," *Union Seminary Quarterly Review* (Fall 1976).

Cowley Publications is a work of the Society of St. John the Evangelist, a religious community for men in the Episcopal Church. The books we publish are a significant part of our ministry together with the work of preaching, spiritual direction, and hospitality. Our aim is to provide books that will enrich their readers' religious experience and challenge it with fresh approaches to religious concerns.